TO LAY A HEARTH

By the same author

The Chinese Ginger Jars

Richer by India

TO LAY
A HEARTH

MYRA SCOVEL

HARPER & ROW, PUBLISHERS

NEW YORK, EVANSTON

AND LONDON

LIBRARY OF CONGRESS CATALOG CARD NUMBER: 68-17581

For Fred
who kept the book
and its writer
in the palms of his hands

TO LAY A HEARTH

I

"I know what you are thinking," I said to my husband. We were sitting on the living room floor, unwrapping the old Mogul bricks from yellowed copies of the Delhi *Statesman*.

"You always know what I'm thinking," he replied. "It's a good thing I haven't got some gorgeous blonde on my mind. But this time you hardly needed extrasensory perception. We are both thinking of Chandru."

Chandru had been our cook during the six years we were medical missionaries in India. We could see his face now as he watched us wrap those dirty, worn bricks in newspaper and pack them in our trunk. The bricks had come from what was said to be the oldest Presbyterian mission church in the world—the church on the compound where we lived in Ludhiana in the Punjab. Some of the original handmade bricks had to be replaced a short time before we were to leave that sun-warmed, color-filled country. Twelve of the ancient tiles would be something tangible to carry home and lay in our own hearth.

"But why not take good new bricks?" Chandru wanted to know. It was hard to explain our sentiment for Mogul tile. He went off shaking his head, the set of his back eloquent: "What would these foreigners do next?" I missed Chandru.

"I wonder what he'd think if he could see his Doctor Sahib in disreputable dungarees, sitting on the floor with a pail of cement between his knees," I said.

"The old boy would be even more surprised if he knew I'd laid this floor myself," Fred replied. "But the hearth is your job. There is something sacramental about laying a hearth. It needs a woman's hand."

"I couldn't possibly do it. I'd have that gooey cement all over everything."

"I'll take care of the cement." He smoothed a layer over the tar paper on the floor. "But you'll have to show me where you want the flagstones and where you want the old bricks."

I knew where every piece should go and began to set out the pattern. These were more than bricks. They were the gold of the Punjab sun, the very dust through which thousands of bronze-brown feet had moved. Streaks of sienna, red, and orange might have dripped from bright saris as they passed. And the marks of the hand that smoothed the clay were still there to be seen—the signature of the artist. Interspersed between the Mogul tiles, I laid the grape-red slabs of flagstone purchased in our own Rockland County.

We sat back on our heels to view our work. It was a suitable hearth for the low-hung brown enamel fireplace-stove which would burn apple logs and pine cones when the children came home for Christmas. Fred unfolded his long legs and went off with his cement to patch a spot in the cellar wall. I sat still, thinking.

What would "home" be like after almost thirty years of living as missionaries in China and India? The word "missionary" meant a lot to us. We were proud to be numbered among that company of idealistic, frustrated (and frustrating!), visionary, hard-working, loving (and beloved!), "kooky" people. Fred, who had healed bodies and taught young Chinese and Indians the art of medicine, would now be an executive. Perish the thought! I, who had been wife, mother, homemaker, and part-time nurse, was about to embark on a "career." Would we fit into this bright, brittle, executive-with-computer age in America, after our years of living in the ancient culture of interior China and in the mellowed civilization of India? There was a lot more to laying a hearth than setting bricks and flagstone into cement.

II

The seaman's strike in Karachi, Pakistan, was the first of the G-wave shocks of our re-entry into America. Suddenly we were no longer members of a minority group, the "Christians," or of an even smaller minority group, the "missionaries." Now we were numbered among the mighty. For Fred and I and our two youngest—Judy, seventeen, and Vicki, fifteen—were four of the Americans on board the Italian ship, *Victoria,* which had sailed from Bombay two days previously, on June 9, 1959. We were Americans. Just that and only that. In a way it felt good; we no longer had to be "shining examples." Instead, passengers from other nations were seeing us as part of that great power structure which was having such an influence upon the future of their countries and upon their individual lives. They were looking at us and asking, "What are they like, these Americans?" not, "What are they like, these missionaries who seem to want to do something for us?"

Our awareness of this inner questioning made us acutely conscious of the other Americans on board. We felt responsible, not only for our own acts, but for everything *they* said and did. We had not realized this when we first boarded the ship and were full of the prospect of reunion with our four older children in America. But America was half a world away; the blood of India was still flowing through our veins. We were looking at our fellow countrymen as Indians might look at them.

India had been an entirely different adventure after our twenty-one years in China, where four of our six children had been born. All of us thought of China as another home country. But the Communists had closed the door firmly behind us. Grieved as we were at the finality of the severing, we could count our blessings. We were all alive and well, after living for six years within the sound of the guns of the Sino-Japanese War and for a year and a half under the Communist regime. When we were finally released, in January, 1951, I wanted nothing less than to settle down in Stony Point, New York, and to remain there forever.

It was not easy for Fred to break the news to me, two summers later, that he felt he must answer the request of the United Church of Northern India to become professor of medicine at the Christian Medical College in Ludhiana.

"I hate to do this to you," he said. "I hate to do this to both of us."

"And to the children," I added.

"That's exactly what I mean. This time we'll have to leave Jim and Carl and Anne here for college."

"We wouldn't see them for six long years. Right now, that seems like a lifetime. And Tom would only have two years with us before he'd have to leave." I did not see how I could possibly go.

But the call was clear to Fred. It was clear enough to me; I simply did not want to answer it. Yet God gradually led us all into the belief that this was His plan for us. He opened the way for my acceptance and made the separations bearable for each of us.

The door had closed on China, and on our home in America. Of our own volition we had opened this new door to India, and we found there color, sun, love, people—friends and experiences I might never have had if I had turned my back on Fred's opportunity. And now, after six years, the door was slowly swinging shut once more.

"Do we always have to be pulling up roots and tearing them out of our hearts?" I thought that last hot day in Bombay.

Judy and Vicki were looking down from the windows of our room in the Airlines Hotel, watching the people on the streets of their beloved India for what might be the last time in their lives. They were finding the parting even more difficult than we.

It came to me as a shock that neither of the girls remembered much about America. Our short furloughs had meant travel, not home. All our thoughts had been geared to the time when we would be going back to the field. "Going back home," the children called it. Even our shopping was done for the year or years ahead. Certainly there was no feeling of permanence during these few months in our home land. When we left America last time, Vicki had only been a bit over ten years old. She, and perhaps Judy, too, could hardly remember the faces of aunts and uncles and friends whom they had seen for such brief periods of time.

"School in the States won't be like Woodstock," said Vicki, feeling my eyes on her back and turning around. "We'll miss Woodstock as much as Tom misses climbing in his Himalayas. He's been in the States three years and he's still writing about it."

"Of course," said Judy, her back still toward us.

"And just think," Vicki added, "I'll never be asked to beetle-sit again."

Every boy at Woodstock School had a three-inch rhinoceros beetle during the rainy season, and lucky the young lady chosen to feed it mangoes and change the leaves in its box while the young man was away for an athletic meet. Vicki's special charge belonged to Nikay Bhukkanasant, a boy from Thailand. After having had friends from twenty-one nations, the girls might find school in America rather dull.

Judy was still at the window. The sun from a side window sprinkled flecks of gold on her red-brown hair. Her deep sigh opened memories of my own teens. Wrapped in the tragedy of the dream that now could never come true, I would not tell her that the object of her dream would be forgotten in a matter of months.

The door banged open and Fred came in with the new suitcase he had gone out to buy—the battered black-and-white had collapsed en route to Bombay. We fell into our usual routine—I handing him clothing, boxes, and household paraphernalia in all the wrong sizes; he packing them without a word. No matter how much I piled beside him, there was a stage at which he would remark, "Is *this* all you have?" The procedure would usually end with, "What do you think this suitcase is, a box car?"

In no time at all he was saying, "There. That's done for one more time." He snapped the suitcase shut as I sat on it. We rarely spoke when packing. It was the only occasion in our lives when we sensed hostility in each other. This uprooted feeling did something to both of us at the same time. We had learned to get the packing done as quickly as possible. Judy and Vicki had learned to leave—to take a walk, to do anything. "We'll be in the lobby if you want us," they'd said.

Now I had my husband back again. "I feel as if I'd come to the end of an era," he said, filling his pipe.

"What do you mean by that?" I asked.

"Everything I came to India to do is done. Let's pray that

Ludhiana will replace me with a good Indian specialist in internal medicine."

As chairman of the Ludhiana Christian Medical College's hospital building committee, he had dug the first shovelful of earth for the hospital foundation. Five of the nine projected blocks, plus the chapel, were now in use. One graduating class had already received the M.B.B.S. degree, the equivalent of an M.D. To help with the upgrading which would enable the college to confer this advanced degree was one reason why Fred had come to India. What pleased him about his new job in New York as Secretary of the Christian Medical Council for Overseas Work, was that he would still be able to work with these students of his, and with other medical students around the world. One small part of his new assignment would be to find residencies and postgraduate opportunities for them in the United States and other countries.

"India is already behind him," I thought, watching him pace the room restlessly. The packing was done; that dreaded tearing apart of friend from friend, which goes by the name of "fare well," was over. He was eager to get back into a routine.

"I wonder which one of the children we'll see first at the dock in New York," said Fred.

"I'll bet it'll be Anne," said Judy, as she and Vicki came through the door. "Or Tom, maybe."

Such a surge of joy welled up within me that I caught my breath. There was nothing between us and our children now except the voyage home! Now we would relax, watch the long green waves, sit with feet up on our deck chairs in the sun.

Or so we thought as we boarded the *Victoria* in Bombay, India, for Karachi, Pakistan, our first port of call.

❧ III ❦

All portents augured well for a perfect voyage home. Vicki knew it was our ship because it was named for her—*Victoria*. It flew the Italian flag, and I claimed an Italian Countess in my ancestry. So much for signs and omens.

And so much for "feet up on our deck chairs in the sun." In that coastal storm between Bombay and Karachi, we had our feet up in berths. The waves were black, not green. *We* were green, I realized, looking across at Judy and Vicki lying in their bunks. The few times we were able to drag ourselves to the rest room (Who was the sadist who concocted the deodorizers for ships' toilets?), we picked up rumors from fellow unfortunates.

"Ships literally breed rumors," I said to Fred when he came in. "I wonder why."

"People are out of touch on shipboard; nothing happens. It's very disquieting to some people to have nothing happen, so to fill the vacuum they pretend that something *is* happening."

"But a seaman's strike? That's a new one."

Judy slid down from her upper berth. I'll go ask Chamez," she said.

"Who on earth is Pajamies?" asked her father.

"Daddy, you would! It's Chamez, our cabin man. He spells it J-A-M-E-S."

"J-A-M-E-S is pronounced 'Chamez'?"

"Of course. How else?" Judy called from the door.

It was an hour before Judy returned. "I had to give him an English lesson," she told us.

"Did you learn anything about the strike?" I asked.

"It's coming off in Pakistan, as soon as we land in Karachi. We're apt to be stuck there forever."

"Oh, why couldn't we have stayed in India?" asked Vicki.

"What will we do for money?" I wanted to know.

"To look at the three of you, anyone would think the end of the world had come!" exclaimed Fred. "Whoever started this rumor will be delighted to have found three such gullible women. Nothing is going to happen. Let's get up on deck and get some fresh air."

We awoke next morning to find the ship on strike in the harbor of Karachi. We three did not say one word as we looked at our husband and father. But he was not deceived. " 'I told you so' is written all over your faces," he assured us—which we, of course, denied.

Relationships were not improved by the announcement over the loudspeaker that there would be no breakfast. Not even coffee? Not even coffee. At ten o'clock, we forgave Fred his optimism when he presented each of us with a boxed lunch, sent in from one of the hotels. "Anyway, Daddy, it was nice not to have to worry about it all night," said Judy. We "breakfasted" on chicken, mutton, ham (in Muslim Pakistan?), bread, fruit, and a small piece of cake.

At noon, we were herded into buses and taken to the Beach Luxury Hotel, where we spent the afternoon waiting in queue after queue in the steaming atmosphere. Lunch was over at last and the buses took us back to the ship.

At ten that night, the first-class passengers called a meeting in the ship's lounge, where "we are going to demand that the

ship sail!" They closed in on the captain like snarling hyenas. Already overwrought by a day of failure in negotiating, the huge man stood, like a bewildered bear, looking from left to right, his "paws" dangling above his paunch.

Fred and I were ashamed at being part of this pack, the most vocal of whom were Americans. The captain was in the humiliating position of having to beg for mercy. He was "given" twenty-four hours. When the company's agent was also thrown into the arena, we walked out. We simply had to take a turn around the deck to "blow our brains fresh."

"I can't understand what happens to Americans when they put a few feet of ocean between themselves and their native shores," I began. "As your mother would have said, 'and they seem like such nice people.' "

"Are we essentially such land creatures that we have to feel our feet on solid ground to be secure?" Fred ventured.

"That may be it. Perhaps they throw their weight around because they are frightened of the unusual."

"Not all Americans throw their weight around. There are the Leighton Stuarts and the Grays and the Doug Formans, the Ned Dodds, and. . . ."

"And the Schmidts and the Chester Bowles and all the rest," I interrupted. "You know I don't lump all businessmen and government officials in one category, nor all tourists either, for that matter. And we both know missionaries who throw their weight around. What I am getting at is that nobody ever speaks of a European or an Oriental, or a Latin American tourist with that deprecating pronunciation of the word. Why does the inflection have to be reserved for Americans?"

"Maybe it bears out my thesis: Europeans are used to traveling. They come from generations of travelers, and they probably don't have the insecurity we have when we leave that huge chunk of ground we call home."

We stopped to watch the reflection of the ship's lights, lying long upon the water.

"You don't throw your weight around," I said.

"I don't have any weight to throw around."

"That's a typical answer, and anything but true. We could go on with *that* particular argument all night. You know, one of the wonderful things about being married to you is that we never get talked out."

"I'll bet we'll be sitting on a cloud a billion years from now, still saying that same thing." He took my arm in his and we began another turn around the deck.

Half way around, he stopped. "You know, this is something we've got to come to grips with."

"What?" I asked.

"We feel like outsiders. We look at our own people as if they were a new breed. We even sit in judgment upon them. I suppose in a way we always have. It's part of living in a democracy, but this seems different."

"I didn't really mean to judge them," I said, unwilling to face his accusations. "I just want to know what makes them tick."

"See? You said 'them,' not 'us.' Maybe we've been international citizens too long."

"We felt terribly American in China, and even more so in India, didn't we?"

"Yes, I guess we did. But now that we are Americans again, we don't feel like Americans."

"Everything is so different. Is any place going to feel like home?"

"Don't be silly. Of course it is. You're tired. Let's go to bed."

Breakfast next morning was an all-time low—two spoiled eggs, a very stale bun, and one cup of lukewarm tea. But the representative from the American Consulate raised the barometer several degrees with the announcement that the Post Exchange would be open to us. We ordered *Coffee*, crackers, cheese, fig newtons, and though our meager funds for the trip through Europe were slowly disappearing, we splurged on a box of Whitman's Sampler chocolates. We hadn't seen one in six years.

Nothing could have been more inert than our ship on strike. Even the air around it was still. If a breeze arose, it approached stealthily, lifted our hair, then let it fall. Our footsteps made separate hollow echoes as we walked the deck that afternoon and evening.

But the next morning, as we rounded a corner, the ship suddenly came alive. The crew, gathered at one side of the prow, let out a shout that sounded like triumph. Was the strike over? We hurried forward. One of the men had landed a fish. It flopped on the deck as helpless as we were. The men were having the time of their lives, in no hurry, apparently, to settle differences.

We spent the rest of that long, hot, boring day at the Beach Luxury Hotel, returning to the ship at 10:00 P.M., in time for another meeting in the lounge. The committee of passengers announced that a cable had been sent through the Italian Consul urging the Italian Government to intervene. (It had already intervened.) Fred helped in making out priority lists for airlifting passengers to their destinations in Europe. Those who were ill and families with children must be flown out first, especially those with small babies really in danger because of the lack of milk and other needed foods. Adults could wait.

Hours passed so very slowly. It was too hot to do anything, even to go to the Beach Luxury Hotel. But food was not a problem, now that the United States Government had come to the rescue and opened to us that heretofore controversial institution, the PX. We felt a little proud that the question had not even arisen whether or not to include the passengers of other nationalities among the favored. All of us were in need, and all of us were given the same opportunity to procure food. Our stock rose considerably, and we Americans were accepted into what became one big unhappy family. We drank our coffee, munched crackers and cheese, opened cans of fruit and passed them around. We swapped rumors, watched our money dwindle, and waited.

❧ IV ❧

"Happy Anniversary." I opened my eyes. Fred was sitting on the edge of Vicki's berth, looking at me. There was no smile on his face. "Are you still glad you married me, even today?"

"I'm still glad I married you, even today," I assured him, though, at this point in our lives, he certainly needed no reassuring. It was the morning of our thirtieth wedding anniversary, June 15, 1959. We were still in Karachi.

"Where are the girls?"

"You shouldn't ask. They're up to something; I'm not sure what."

We kept looking at one another. Could it be possible that thirty years had passed since that wedding morning? If this was not a typical, traditional way to spend one's thirtieth wedding anniversary, there had been nothing typical or traditional about that other morning, either. At this hour the bride had been having breakfast in bed—in the groom's house! Her mother-in-law-to-be had no sooner set the tray on a bedside table than the groom appeared at the door in his pajamas, coffee cup in hand.

"Frederick Gilman Scovel," gasped his mother. "What will our house guests think? Go back to your room, *please*."

"What's so terrible about my being here?" He came over to help himself from the pile of toast on my tray. "Now, Mother, you don't really think the few words Father will say

in another few hours will make all that difference, do you?"
he added, sitting down on the foot of my bed.

"Frederick, what has come over you! You never used to be
this way!"

Fred kept on with his teasing. "It's all because of this
woman you've taken into your house."

"It's too late to do anything about it now," I told him.
"Get out! Or your bride will have to walk down the aisle in
her negligee."

My father met me at the church door. "Oh, Daddy, I'm so
glad you're here," I said as he hugged me hard. "I don't know
what I'd do without you today."

"You wouldn't even be here today if it weren't for me." He
tucked my hand under his arm and we started down the long
aisle that became a path across the world—to Karachi, Pakistan, in fact.

"It *was* a wonderful wedding wasn't it?" mused Fred,
though I hadn't said a word aloud. He picked up his shaving
things and began to lather his face at the mirror above the
cabin washstand. "Do you remember the photo Bill Wall
hung on your bulletin board at the hospital when we became
engaged?"

Bill Wall, one of the doctors at Cortland County Hospital
where Fred and I were working, had found a newspaper clip-
ping advertising gas furnaces. A beautiful bride was throwing
her bouquet from an elegant staircase. The caption read,
"Whoever thought *she'd* shovel coal?"

"Whoever thought *she'd* spend her thirtieth wedding anniversary in the harbor of Karachi?" said Fred out of half his
mouth as he shaved one cheek.

A shuffle at the door, and the tinkle of glassware and dishes
—Judy and Vicki were surprising me with breakfast in bed.
Fred was to have his on a chair beside me. Notes on our trays
read, "You will have your anniversary present when we get to

Europe." Not *"if* we get to Europe," but *"when* we get to Europe." It set the tone for the day and we spent it in hope, packing.

At four o'clock the girls, back from their language session with "Chamez," threw open the door, singing "Happy Anniversary to You." They were followed by two of the dearest Americans anywhere in the world—two young women out to see the world "before we settle down to old maidhood"—Jean and Carolyn Something-or-other were carrying a beautifully decorated cake. This time we really *were* surprised.

"Where on earth did you find it?" we asked.

"Product of the Beach Luxury Hotel," Jean announced. "Bless their hearts, I didn't know they had anything but cold chicken."

"Please don't say those words," said Carolyn. "I don't even want to think 'cold chicken' again."

The surprises were not yet over. We had hardly cut the cake before we heard a knock at the door. It was a man from the purser's office who asked, "Family Scovel, will you go tonight?"

Would we go tonight? Would we ever! But Fred said, "We can wait. There are still mothers with small children who should go first, as we have said before."

Either the officer did not understand or he did not choose to understand. He simply repeated the question, "Family Scovel, will you go tonight?"

"But why us, instead of some of the others?" Fred pursued.

No answer was given. The question was repeated once more. *"Will* you go tonight?"

"We will go," Fred answered at last.

"This is your anniversary present from God," said Vicki. "At least it wasn't another white purse. Remember when we were small, we could never think of anything nicer to give you than a new white handbag or purse?"

"And one was never enough; we each had to give you one," said Judy.

"I spent my life changing things from one white bag to another, for fear you'd think I liked one better than the other," I confessed. "Those bags never wore out. The bottom drawer was always full of them and I didn't dare give one away."

"Come on, girls. Don't just stand there. We're on our way to Europe," said Fred.

It was midnight before we had signed all the papers the purser had given us, and completed the arrangements for moving the luggage. Miraculously, we found a taxi to take us to the airlines office for what we thought would be a routine check-in. We would pick up the tickets bought for us by the Lloyd Triestino Line and still have time to catch the one-thirty flight for Rome.

The Pakistani agent frowned. "I thought I had told those people that there is no flight to Rome tonight. You will have to go back to the ship and wait until they get you a flight."

"We can't go back to the ship," said Fred.

"Why?" we all asked at once.

"Because I had to sign a document saying that all our transactions with the ship were completed and we would not come back under any circumstances."

"What will we do now?" I asked the agent.

He shifted heavily from one foot to the other, then picked up the airlines guide and ran a thick finger down the page. "There's a flight to Zurich, Switzerland, in an hour. We'll have to hurry if you want reservations."

"We'll take them," Fred said. "That's near enough to pick up *some* transportation to Rome."

Even with the two agents working as fast as they could write, sign, and fold, I thought those four tickets would never be made out. At last the envelope was in Fred's hands. "That will be two hundred fifty-two United States dollars more than the tickets paid for by the steamship company," he said, smiling. I was about to burst into tears. "Why, what's the matter?" he asked.

The matter was that we had less than one-fourth that amount to get us to Naples, where the Mennonite travel agency would meet us with hotel reservations, railway tickets, and the travel money we had deposited with them for the three weeks in Europe. We couldn't go back to the ship. We could not use our few dollars for a hotel room. What were we to do?

Long ago we had learned that when we reached an impasse, it was wise to wait it out. The Pakistani agent and his assistant had not one word of complaint about the trouble it had been to prepare the tickets to Zurich. Fred and he began to talk about labor problems and strikes in general. The assistant took Judy and Vicki into the back room to show them how the teletype machine worked. I sat in one of the imitation leather chairs and pondered the strangeness of my thirtieth wedding anniversary.

"It was lots of fun," said Judy when the girls returned. "We watched him type a message to London. He used that old typing exercise, 'The quick brown fox jumped over the lazy dog' and the reply came back, 'We do not understand your message. Please repeat.' He had to think fast. He told London he thought the machine was broken, but that everything seemed okay now."

"I think I'll work for an airline when I graduate from college," said Vicki. They each picked a chair and were soon asleep. A long silence settled over the dust of the waiting room. Only the buzz of voices could be heard from what seemed miles away, as Fred and the agent continued their discussions.

Suddenly, the street door banged open and a prosperous-looking American all but fell into the room. He made unsteady progress toward the counter and leaned against it.

"Ish thish an airlines offish, or ishn't it?" he demanded.

"Yes, sir. This is the central airlines office. What can I do for you, sir?" asked the agent.

"Oh, it ish, ish it?" He pounded a fist on the desk, swung back his top coat and pulled an envelope from his hip pocket. "What I want to know ish, ish thish an airlines offish or ishn't it?"

"Yes, sir. It is. What do you want, sir?"

We longed to tell our fellow-countryman that sarcasm, even with the accompanying sneer, does not come across in another language. Ultimately, the agent learned that the man had three tickets on a flight to Istanbul, leaving at two-thirty that very morning. What he wanted was a direct flight to Rome. When he found that no direct flight was available, he plunked his three tickets down on the counter and demanded his money back. He was immediately reimbursed, and he soon reeled out of the office.

Fred had joined me, leaving the agents with their client. While the girls slept, we two stood disconsolately under the naked bulbs of the wheel chandelier, watching the reactions of our Pakistani friends. One would have thought that they had seen enough of Americans for one night. Instead, they were elated. The heavier one, with the black curly hair, motioned for us to come to the desk.

"Here are three tickets on the next plane for Istanbul." He was all but dancing with delight. "One of the young ladies may ride in the seat reserved for the stewardess. That will take care of the four of you. From Istanbul you can pick up a plane for Rome in an hour or two at the most. And the price is exactly the same as the steamship pays for you."

"Girls," I called, running across to them, "We've had

another anniversary present!"

But whether it was from the persistent Italian from the purser's office, our inebriated fellow American, the Pakistani agents, or from God, I did not know. I looked up through the wheel chandelier and thanked The Latter. Now we were really on our way.

V

"At least the taxi was able to find the place," said Fred, as we and our luggage spilled out of the ancient vehicle into the streets of Rome. "It's risky business asking an airlines baggage clerk to recommend a pension."

"But what else could you have done?" I asked.

"I'll be glad when we get to Naples and catch up with that itinerary packet from the travel agency." He counted out lire with the help of the taxi driver, who drove off so cheerfully that Fred decided to study the currency of the country a little more thoroughly.

The moment we opened the door of that small hotel, I felt panic. An overwhelming aura of evil permeated the dark halls, an evil so tangible I could almost touch it. In our room, we were all very quiet. Fred began to unpack.

"Please, wait a minute," I said.

"Why? What's the matter?"

"There's something terribly wrong with this place." He waited, and I finally blurted out, "Darling, you'll hate me for this, but could we possibly look for another hotel?"

"You and your intuitions! What's wrong with this one?"

"Nothing—I guess."

"Well, something is bothering you. What is it?"

"I don't know," I said, feeling like a fool. "It isn't anything I can see or even tell about. It's just a sense of evil so strong that I'm afraid. I'm sorry, I really am, but I just can't explain it."

"Now listen, sweetheart, you're tired. We're all tired. Let's get to bed."

"Not here, Daddy, *please*," begged Judy. "I feel it, too. It's terrifying."

"Well, Vicki, how about you?" he asked.

"Looks okay to me," she replied, "a little dingy, spooky maybe, but—"

"*Please?*" Judy and I pleaded in one breath.

Without another word, Fred snapped his briefcase shut, shoved it under his armpit, picked up the two heaviest suitcases and started toward the door. We followed sheepishly—I feeling ashamed, but unable to say "Come back. It will be all right."

Just around the corner, we found a pension as happy as the other had been ominous, with a waiter at breakfast who began at once to teach us Italian, improve Fred's knowledge of the currency, and tell us what we should see. Adding to our sense of security, a policeman and his wife from Los Angeles were seated at the next table. In no time at all we were chatting away about our families and why we were in Rome. It was so good to meet a stranger and to be able to talk to him in our own language, without the fear of riding roughshod over another culture. Remembering that the policeman was on vacation, I did not mention the mystery of the horror-filled hotel. In the bright sun of a new day in this delightful country, I wondered if I had dreamed it. But Judy hadn't dreamed it, too. The mystery remained unsolved.

"The first thing we do this morning is buy you a new nightgown, Mom," she said.

"Well, I should hope so," said Vicki. "I couldn't take another night of looking at that billious green seersucker."

"I'm furious every time I put it on," I admitted.

The villain of the story behind the seersucker nightgown was a cow. I had accepted the cows in India, even on that rainy day when a herd of them wandered in from the street and made an Augean stable of our front patio. One got used to seeing no bit of landscape without one or two or ten cows in it. One waited while the traffic got unsnarled as they wandered about the city streets; one was no longer shocked when a shopkeeper allowed them to devour a good share of his fresh vegetables; and one patiently restored the damage when a flower garden had been reduced to shambles.

Considered sacred by our Hindu friends, cows were certainly not to be molested by us who were guests in the country. May heaven forbid that any devout Hindu was near enough to read my thoughts the afternoon that one of those beasts ate my last nightgown. It was a soft, pink nylon that I had been saving for the trip home and had only worn my last few days in Ludhiana. The day before we left, I had washed it and spread it across the hedge to dry quickly before putting it into a suitcase. Returning to pick it up, I saw the last pink shred disappearing into the mouth of a cow. I chased that animal back into the street, banged shut the gate through which it had entered, and sat down in the garden to cry in exasperation.

Noel Matheson, an English girl on the staff of the Medical College, came to my rescue—as Noel had a way of doing—with the gift of one of her nightgowns. But the dainty sprigged seersucker was now much the worse for too many dryings in the Pakistan sun.

Vicki picked out an ice-blue nylon from the many in the Rome department store. Judy pronounced it "pretty, but not very private." But the time was within sight when I would own more than one nightgown.

"I'm warning you, I'm going to ask for a new one every Christmas and every birthday," I told Fred when we stopped by for him at the book stall.

Rome was a strange alchemy of holy day and holiday. Holiday breathed into ancient holy rites and made them alive. Holiness became part of the breath of holiday until the whole city had an air of continuous Easter.

As we walked the streets, we found it difficult not to stop every American we saw. And we were amazed that they could pass us by so casually. We had to remember that Rome, although in a foreign country, was nothing like the interior cities in which we had lived in the Orient. If an American, or any foreigner, appeared in our Shantung city he needed our help—a place to spend the night, an American meal, a paperback to tuck in his knapsack, a chance to talk about his adventures or to ask directions to further ones. He might be a writer, a buyer of furs, an archaeologist, a refugee, one of a United Nations Survey team, a well digger, or a student traveling on a budget consisting solely of youth. He was sure to be lonely. Here in Rome, Americans traveled in bevies.

"There isn't an American here who even flicks an eyelash as we pass," said Fred. "There isn't one who needs a good hot bath in a real bathtub."

At Naples, we were finally handed those thrilling pages of literature entitled, "Menno Travel Service, Final Itinerary, Dr. Frederick G. Scovel and Family." We came to appreciate the words "Two blocks from the station" following the names of some of the hotels, since we were not able to afford taxis or porters. Money for such luxuries lay in the tills of the Beach Luxury Hotel in Pakistan.

We learned how to use the continental breakfast, consisting of beverage and rolls, already paid for as part of the hotel bill. We ordered coffee and cocoa and mixed half a cup of each. This "mocha" not only woke us up but gave us the calories we needed to walk through the miles of museums we felt we must see. At night we looked for small restaurants without tourists and ordered what we saw the patrons eating. It was usually spaghetti, which Vicki would deftly twirl on her spoon as she watched what was going on around her, oblivious until the spaghetti was neatly wound up the handle of her fork and onto her hand.

Switzerland was all the beautiful calendars we had ever seen of it, and more. Switzerland was Zurich and Sister Toni.

We had known Sister Toni Mueller in Tsining, China. She had been a nurse in the Basel Mission Hospital across the city from us. We were delighted to be with her now in her own home in Zurich. Her sister Marthe fed us Rahm Schnitzel, fresh strawberries, and her special recipe for Bircher Muesli. While Fred questioned their brother on population and industry, Toni and I reminisced.

"Remember the night during the Japanese occupation when I was leaving your house late? You were worried for fear I would be in danger, and I said, 'Never fear, I shall scream.' Then I showed you what I would do in an emergency."

"We almost had an emergency then and there," I recalled. "I will never forget that scream. The Japanese soldiers came running from all over the south suburb."

"As I remember it, Fred explained that I often had these screaming spells, but that he was a doctor and knew I would be all right in a few minutes," said Toni. "And you, Judithle, I remember the day you were born."

"What did she look like?" asked Vicki.

"She was the most beautiful baby I have ever seen," Toni replied.

"Too bad she ever grew up," said Vicki.

Judy gave her the usual "your-hour-is-at-hand" look.

"You brought us vegetables from your garden when the

Japanese guards wouldn't let us go out," I said. "It was dangerous for you, Toni."

"Those were wonderful days," she said, and sighed.

Wonderful days! We were in danger hourly. Gunfire was our background music. We were without money and food, caught behind enemy lines, unable to return to our homelands; but they were days to hold in grateful remembrance. Why? I thought about it on the lake that afternoon. Perhaps the days were wonderful because we were completely helpless to do anything about the situation and so were thrown back upon God, utterly dependent upon Him. It must be true that prayer opens to us a richer experience than we have when we can manage easily on our own. What would that mean in terms of our life in America, where everything we could wish for was available?

Surely, our remembrances were treasured because of friends like Toni, who could easily have claimed her neutrality and remained across the city, safe in her Swiss-related hospital, and who now treated her heroism as if it hadn't existed.

Only the anticipation of a trip through the Black Forest to Heidelberg made it possible for us to tear ourselves away. Switzerland would mean to us not only the grandeur of snow-filled crags piercing the sky; it would also mean the clean, fresh smell of Marthe's kitchen and the sanctity of memories. Europe was proving to be a strange combination of our past and the future we would be finding in America. I was glad now, that we had not flown directly home from India.

"I love Switzerland," said Vicki. "I'm coming back here on my honeymoon, if I have to come alone."

Ah, romantic Heidelberg! We stepped off the bus into a downpour of rain. Stiff with fatigue and groggy from the cigar smoke in the bus, we could hardly remember the storybook beauty through which we had been driving all day. We slopped through the streets, carrying the heavy suitcases, searching for the hotel. Our progress was further slowed by Judy who insisted upon walking a block behind us "so she could be alone." In our room at last, we pulled back the curtains for a look at a castle or the ancient towers of the University and saw only a vista of sooty roofs, with a foreground of somebody's pants sagging on a line.

At dinner that night, we were surrounded by tourists—loud, unpleasant, demanding.

"What's the matter with this place that ya can't get Sand Mills, Iowa, by phone? Just keep tryin' till ya get it."

"Yeah, but how much is it in *real* money?"

"Are you going to wear your shorts when we go out for beer?"

"Ethel! ETHEL!"

"Okay, okay, I'm COMING."

"Let's get out of here," said Judy, before she had finished her rice pudding. "Somebody might think we were Americans."

"I don't see how," said Vicki.

Fred looked across at me, shrugged helplessly, and got up. We hurried back to our rooms, closed the curtains on the dejected laundry, and went to bed.

It was still raining when we boarded the steamer at Mainz for the trip to Koblenz. But it was impossible to feel the charm of the German Rhineland, because the steamer, too, had a full capacity of tourists. Above the noise of the propellers, Bob Somebody was shouting into a microphone, taping a broadcast for his hometown radio. First he interviewed two Yorkshiremen on what they thought of the trip; then described each castle along the way, stopping only long enough for the tape recorder to pick up the music of *Die Lorelei,* which the ship played as we passed the famous rocks. We did not see, much less have the opportunity to speak with, one German that whole day.

By now, we were too tired to enjoy anything, and the fault was our own. When we planned our itinerary, we suspected that we were cramming in too much, but how could we leave anything out? We could not fail to see the works of art we had studied with the children in the Calvert Course—the *Discus Thrower,* the *Boy Pulling out a Thorn, Laocoön, the Pietà,* the bronze doors by Ghiberti, the Botticellis, the Fra Angelicos, the Ghirlandajos—and certainly not *La Scala!*

Leaving Fred and Vicki to photograph Milan, Judy and I went off to see that magnificent red velvet opera house. Alone in the concert hall, we heard a piano solo backstage. Or was it the accompaniment for ballet practice? We could hear distinctly the thata-thata-thata-thum of ghostly feet. It had been a highlight of our trip. Suppose we had left it out?

But in Heidelberg we realized that although we could swallow Europe in one gulp, we could not possibly digest it. In fact, we were having a good case of acid something-or-other right now. We would rest for a day and take Paris much easier.

Paris was Vicki's idea. Her only interest in Europe was to see the city from the top of the Eiffel Tower. Our day's allowance restricted us to only one trip on the scenic elevator, but Fred, Judy, and I were delighted to sit on a bench in the sun and "talk" to the French children and their parents. Vicki came back radiant.

We hurried to the little Impressionist exhibition across from the Louvre. The Louvre was out of bounds. "If I have to look at one more nude statue, I'll scream louder than Sister Toni," Vicki warned us.

"She's not kidding," Judy whispered to me.

"Okay, honey, no more sculpture," I promised.

"And no more museums," said her father. "We'll be seeing Brother Li in Holland on Sunday. That ought to make you both happy."

✦ VI ✦

Brother Li, a lay brother in the Roman Catholic Order, The Society of the Divine Word, started his own ecumenical movement in China in 1931. It may well have been earlier, but 1931 was the year the Scovel family met him. Brother Li would laugh at the idea of his having started a movement. Certainly there was no studied "dialogue" between us. We were friends, and as friends we were interested in everything that happened to one another. If the happening was a spiritual experience, it was discussed as freely as any other. Brother Li simply kept the door open between his own robust German self and everyone he met. There was not a Chinese shopkeeper, water carrier, ricksha puller, or policeman in the city who did not know him, respect him, and laugh in anticipation of one of his jokes as soon as he came in sight.

Once, and I believe only once, I hurt Brother Li terribly. A few days after the Japanese Army had taken our city, he called to see how we had fared during the battle. Knowing that Germany and Japan were allies, I greeted him with, "Good morning, beloved enemy." For the first time in our years of friendship, a shadow crossed his jovial face.

"Please, *please,*" he said very seriously, "never call me by that terrible word, 'enemy.' "

"I'm sorry," I said. "You know that no matter what happens, we can never think of you as an enemy."

"But I do not want to hear that word from your lips—from anyone's lips. After I fought through the horrible first world war, I vowed I would never again allow myself to be in a position where I could be called an enemy. I am the enemy of no man."

"Of course you're not. I'm *so* sorry. I wouldn't have hurt you for anything in the world."

"I know you wouldn't. I shouldn't have mentioned it. So let's forget all about it. Okay?" He had been speaking in Chinese. All our conversations were in that language since we did not know any German, nor he any English, with the sole exception of the word "okay." (Brother Li loved to say it "in American.")

"Run out and feel my donkey's belly," he said. "Take the two boys and my little Anne with you. Okay? They will find something there."

The "donkey" was Brother Li's bicycle, and the "donkey's belly," the triangular leather case he had made at his shoemaker's bench to hold the accumulations of his many errands for the monastery.

"Where's the doctor?" asked Brother Li, "I thought he would be home for lunch."

"He's still at the hospital. Shall I have the gateman call him?"

"Don't trouble Brother Chang. I'll run over while you are patting the donkey. I need some drugs from the pharmacy, and we may have to arrange for an X-ray for the old Father I told Doctor about last time. I'll come back with him when he comes home. Okay?" The Santa Claus smile was back where it belonged.

This time the "donkey's belly" held sweets for the children. Later, during the Sino-Japanese War, it carried needed food—lentils and blood sausages, smuggled past the guards at our gate.

God sent Brother Li to us in another emergency. When
Fred was wounded by a drunken soldier, Brother Li arrived
at the last hour when it was still possible to get word out to
the American Consul for medical help—badly needed, since
Fred was the only foreign-trained doctor in an area of five
million people. Thanks to Brother Li, a doctor arrived.

We had not seen our friend for years. When all foreigners
were expelled from China, he had been sent to the Society's
monastery in the Netherlands. We could not plan a trip to
Europe without including a visit to Mission House St.
Michael in Steyl.

On that hot Sunday afternoon, the train pulled into the
station at Roermond. Passengers with heads out of windows
to catch the breeze were greeted with a sight which must have
puzzled them. A heavy, white-bearded monk, running down
the platform as if to be first at a fire, had suddenly braked
before this man, his wife, and two teen-aged daughters descending the train steps.

We all tried to embrace Brother Li at the same moment
that he was holding the four of us in one big hug. His welcome was a veritable explosion of Chinese. "Did you have a
good trip? You must be hungry. Come this way to the car.
Father Superior sent it for you. How long has it been since
we have seen each other? Girls! How you have grown! Judy,
don't trip over that suitcase. Now, Mrs. Scovel, up these
stairs. Remember the day I first came to your house and
played with Jim and Carl? Where are the boys now? And how
is my little golden-haired Anne? *Married!* I can't believe it.
Here's the car. Doctor, we'll take the front seat."

A dam of pent-up conversation had broken. The flow of
Chinese never ceased during the several miles of our journey
to the monastery; nor, except for the few hours we were
asleep, did it lessen during our two days' visit. There were

occasional impediments that the stream of language had to by-pass. Mr. George Fring, at whose home we were staying, spoke Dutch and German. Mrs. Fring spoke only Dutch, so all our translating had to be done by Brother Li through the medium of Chinese.

After supper at the monastery that first night, we gathered in the Fring living room. To the accompaniment of Dutch television, Brother Li continued telling us the story he had started at the refectory.

"So I said to the guard at the gate, 'Have you ever actually seen a foreign devil?' And he said, 'Well, no, I . . .' "

"What is he saying?" asked Judy. (Vicki was lost in the television performance.)

"I'll tell you later," I whispered back.

Just then, a voluptuous blonde appeared on the TV screen, singing. I wondered what Brother Li would do. He glanced casually in her direction and addressed her in Chinese. "Ah, so *you* have come, have you? Well, just sit down quietly. I haven't seen these friends in a long time, and I don't want to be interrupted."

The blonde did not sit down quietly, but Brother Li was undaunted. "So I told the guard, 'You will see foreign devils —thousands of them—if you insist upon inspecting these trunks.' There wasn't a thing in them, of course, except the clothing of the new priests just coming out from Germany. 'So,' I said, 'are you willing to take the responsibility for opening these trunks and letting a whole batch of foreign devils loose on the countryside?' 'Okay, okay. Go on with your trunks,' they said. The guards always enjoyed our jokes together."

Oh, it was good to be with our friend once more! We had heard this same story often in the past; it seemed like old times to be hearing it again. Mrs. Fring set glasses of tea before each of us, and while Brother Li was drinking his, she asked her husband a question in Dutch. He referred the question to Brother Li in German, who asked Fred in Chinese, *"T'a men hsien tsai to ta sui shu?"*

"How old *are* you two now?" asked their father, in English. Their reply went back to Mrs. Fring—English to Chinese to German to Dutch. And so the conversation went, through several television shows.

Mrs. Fring finally stood up and let us know by signs that she realized we must want to go to bed. She took us into what was obviously their bedroom, and Judy and Vicki into the only other bedroom in their dear little home. When we went back into the hall to say good-night to Brother Li, Fred took him aside to ask where the Frings would sleep. "Don't worry about these good people. Okay?" he replied.

I couldn't worry long; their bed was too comfortable. The next morning I awoke early and thought about the night before. What a strange evening it had been, this blending of our old life and the new life to come. It had been almost eight years since I had thought in Chinese, and listening to Chinese with a German accent took some concentration, the kind of concentration I found almost impossible with television in the same room. We had not seen a set in six years.

Could it have been only eight years ago that we saw our first television? We had arrived on the West Coast in 1951, after our term in China, the last two years of which had been spent under the Communists. Our release had been like breaking out of a cocoon and seeing light for the first time. Back in America, we found almost every home plunged in darkness!

Visiting Fred's doctor cousin, we learned that television had swept the country during our absence. We sat in a pitch-black room, all eyes fixed on the pictures flickering across the small blob of light before us. Why, we could actually see

what happened, *while it was happening! Incredible!* We
could not tear ourselves away, and there was no incentive to
do so when no one else moved either. Each program was
more fascinating than the last. But as the hours wore on, I
began to wonder if I wanted all these people in my living
room all day and half the night.

During a commercial, Fred asked a question. "Phil, these
things must be pretty expensive. How does a dermatologist in
this country make enough money for all this?"

"What do you mean?" asked Phil.

"I wouldn't think dermatology would pay here," Fred replied. "You certainly don't see the skin diseases we see in
Asia—scabies, ringworm, pemphigus—the works."

"No, of course we don't," said Phil, "at least not in the
amount you see them. But in this country we have a new
source of income—allergies to detergents. You should see the
hands that I see every day since the new detergents have
entered the picture."

What were detergents?

Detergents had completely revolutionized my housekeeping that furlough. I wondered what we ever did without
them. What would be new this time? Universal television,
probably. With my one-thing-at-a-time mind, how was I
going to cope with it as a background to living? The problem
would have to be solved later. I could hear Mrs. Fring in the
kitchen.

"Fred, it's time to get up," I said to his back.

The monastery we saw that day had the tranquillity of
separate still pictures—the huge cross of bright-colored flowers planted against a hill; the underground grotto with surprisingly beautiful figures of the stations of the cross; the
interior of the church, built and decorated by the brothers
and priests, even to the stained glass windows; and one old

priest sitting quietly while a chicadee ate seeds from his cupped hand.

Action returned during our walk through the village. Brother Li introduced us and told the story of our lives to every shopkeeper. He bought chocolates for the girls and wanted to buy everything for us. We held him down to a weather indicator made at the mission printing house. It would hang just inside the door of our new home.

"The pants of the little Dutch boy will turn different colors to let you know of any change in the weather," explained Brother Li. "See how it reads?"

> *Violett: veränderlich*
> *Blau: schön, heiter, trocken*
> *Rot: trübe, regnerisch oder nebelig*

If the weather behaved in America, I might be able to learn to read the indicator by watching what happened outside when the Dutch boy's pants changed from *blau* to *rot*.

"I want to do something for my little Anne," Brother Li said on our last afternoon. "I've been thinking. You say they have no children; this is so sad. Do you think she would like it if we asked the Rose Sisters to pray for her?"

"She'd be delighted that you thought of it," said Fred. "Who are the Rose Sisters?"

"They are an Order for Perpetual Prayer," Brother Li replied. "Day and night, year in and year out, there are always two sisters at the altar praying. Would you like to go to see them? The convent is not far from here. I could ask permission."

"We'd love to," I said. "Then we can tell Anne all about it."

"Okay. Okay. Sit here by the flowers while I go and ask." He sailed off, his cassock billowing. In no time at all, he was hurrying back across the grass, talking long before we could hear him. ". . . and it's okay for you to see them. There are two Chinese sisters there, and Mother Superior thought you might like to meet them. Her representative will be there to greet you. She speaks very good English."

Behind the handwrought iron grill of the convent entrance hall stood the representative in black, with her two little Chinese nuns, one on either side of her. They were wearing the soft rose-colored habit. Brother Li asked them to pray for the daughter of his friends and again, with unabated enthusiasm, told the story of our lives when we worked together in China.

"Tsining? Did you say Tsining? In Shantung Province?" asked one of the nuns. "That was my home."

As we talked back and forth in Chinese, Mother Superior's representative looked from one to the other of her two young charges, happy in their joy. At last Fred reminded us that we must leave; we had barely time to catch the bus for Venlo. We found, when we said good-by, that those few moments at the convent, reaching back into our common past, now swelled through the present and on into the future, friendship never being a matter of time.

It was so, too, when we thanked the Frings for their loving hospitality, a hospitality no less warm for their puzzlement at this strange Protestant family and its relationship to their dear Brother Li.

By the time we began our sightseeing in the Netherlands, we were tourists with no apologies, not even to ourselves. It didn't trouble us at all that the Dutch in the fishing village of Volendam were in "national costume" for our sakes. That was the way Holland *should* look. We joined the throng of Americans snapping photos of old men smoking long pipes and young women selling wooden shoes. We marveled at the

lowlands reclaimed from the sea—smiled at the Dutch prov-
erb, "God made the world, but the Dutch made Holland."

We got out of the bus at the proper place to buy Edam
cheeses, and there was a windmill— a windmill that Vicki
would never forget. All set to snap her photo, she decided she
could get a better angle from the "little green path"
through the field below. She jumped down to try it. Alas for
Vicki, the little green path was an algae-covered, slime-filled
irrigation ditch! And alas for the Dutch housewife who had
to clean up her barn after us! While Vicki shivered from
reaction and cold, I removed her clothes, scrubbed them and
put them back on her, wet. As we tried to thank the helpful
housewife, she eyed us up and down in disgust. She did not
even have to say aloud that word of contempt, "tourists."

Now if I could only fall asleep in Rotterdam and wake up
in New York with all our children around us, how perfect it
would be! And that is just about what happened, due to a
rough voyage and the pills Fred gave me because I was sea-
sick. The Dutch on board the *Ryndam* called it *zeeziekte*.
How they could say that word when they were in that condition was more than I could fathom.

VII

July 20, 1959. At last! At long last we were all but there! Our chests would probably hold permanent indentations from pressing against the rail to hasten the ship forward. As the *Ryndam* swung lazily into port, we searched the dock for our children, wondering again which one we would see first. The gangplanks were lowered leisurely, impervious to our impatience. Still no sign of the children. A man with a sheaf of papers in his hand stepped up to Fred and asked, "You're the Scovels? Welcome home. I'm John La Forte. I have Fred Neuhauser's letter here, and I've come down to help you with your baggage."

"But where are the children?" I asked.

"Oh, they're here all right—about a thousand of them—but they can't come into the customs shed, you know."

We had completely forgotten that the formalities of customs came before seeing anyone from shore. Bless United Presbyterian headquarters for sending someone to help us, and bless John La Forte, pastor of a Presbyterian church in Brooklyn, who did this for incoming missionaries as a way of showing he believed in what they were doing. "Right this way," he said. "We'll have you finished in no time at all."

That squeal could only come from Anne. And of the six, only Anne would refuse to acknowledge the existence of a barrier. Oh, how good her arms felt! I held her off to look at her and she flew into her father's arms, then darted like a humming bird into the arms of each of her sisters and back to me.

"Come on, hurry. You've got to meet my John," she said. "Mother, you'll love him."

Her eyes were greener than I had remembered, her hair in short curls close to her head. "Anne, you look wonderful," I said.

"Do you like my new dress?" She glanced down at her figure in trim navy blue, swung the white stole into a pose and said, "I made it myself, especially for your coming."

"No wonder you got past the customs official," said Fred.

The endless process of examining the luggage was over at last. We hurried to meet the other members of our family. The customs official grinned when Anne flashed the radiance of her joy across him as she passed. "Thank you *so* much," she said. "I haven't seen them in six years. Aren't they wonderful?"

Now we were out in the sunlight, our children running toward us, the strength of their arms enfolding us. I suddenly wondered, who were we to be so loved? We were caught up in a blur of joy as we went from one to the other. Anne's tall, bronze-haired John was just as I thought he would be; Carl's wife, Faith, far more delicately beautiful than her photographs had shown. Both of them seemed to feel as if they had always belonged to this family.

As usual, everyone was talking at once. Tom finally got my ear. "Mom, Uncle Bob is waiting to see you."

"Where?"

"Over by the post."

It was like my understanding brother not to intrude on the family reunion. There he stood, waiting patiently with his two youngest—Betsy, her black curls glistening, and Jim (my, he'd grown!).

"I couldn't help thinking of Dad just now," said Bob, after the hugs all around. "Remember how all five of us used to run to meet him every night when he came home from the mill?"

"And how he'd call to the neighbors on their porches and say . . ."

" 'Somebody must have kicked the hive.' " We said it together and laughed.

"Dorothy and Bob junior couldn't make it," said Bob, "but we'll see you up home in a few days. Think you can manage it, Fred?"

"We wouldn't miss it for the world. We got your letter and are planning on it. I'll give you a ring as soon as we get sorted out here."

Telephones! We'd have telephones! We could call the children long-distance. We could speak to them, hear their voices whenever we wanted to! What a wonderful country we had come home to!

And what glorious pandemonium!

"Mom, Anne's teasing me again," from sedate newspaperman, Jim.

"*I'm* teasing *him?* John, make my brother leave me alone."

Jim's chuckle was never more than an audible smile. I hadn't heard it for six long years.

"Come on, kids, break it up," said their Uncle Bob. "Let's get the show on the road. I've got to get back to the bank."

Groans, and promises to see one another more often. "Thanks so much for driving all the way down for these few minutes," said Fred.

We walked to the car with him. "Bob, have you found us a house?" I asked.

"Of course not. You don't buy houses for other people, and you don't buy a house like you buy eggs at the supermarket. Fred, I thought maybe you'd knocked some sense into her head by this time."

"I've tried. Heaven knows, I've tried," said Fred.

"You conservative bankers make me sick," I said to Bob, and he grinned.

"We'll talk about houses when you come. 'Bye now."

('Bye, now. That was new. I'd never heard him say that before. We'd have to keep our ears open for the new colloquialisms.)

"Give my love to Dorothy and Bobby," I called out. " 'Bye." I didn't dare to say, " 'Bye, now," until I learned whether or not this was just my brother's way of saying it.

"Isn't it wonderful to have real relatives?" said Judy as they drove off.

"Real aunts and uncles and cousins, think of it!" said Vicki, tying her ponytail. Tom had been quietly loosening it. "Missionary aunts and uncles are nice but there's something very special about having *real* ones. Aren't Betsy and Jimmy adorable?"

"Blood is thicker than water," I quoted my mother.

The chaos continued as we decided who should ride with whom on the trip to Leonia, New Jersey, the home of Esther and Hugh Fitch, parents of Anne's John. Esther Fitch could have plotted the campaigns of an army with "no trouble at all." And she could have amply fed *two* armies, her own and the enemy's, while Hugh provided for it—and on the salary of a university professor.

There were hours of good talk ahead for us, I knew. I wanted to ask Hugh about the book of sonnets he was having published. Fred would have carpentry questions for Esther, who was redoing her kitchen alone! Most of all I wanted to thank them for making a home for our children during vacations from college. I wondered if they had any idea of how much it had meant to us on Christmas morning in India to think of our children's being together on that Holy Birthday. But now the Fitches had left us alone on the front veranda.

I looked from one of our brood to the other. Jim was older,

quiet as usual, still "the only quiet Scovel." Carl was
amusedly parrying a barrage of questions on Unitarianism
thrust at him by United Presbyterian minister John, Fred
adding an occasional aside. (Carl was a Unitarian minister, as
was Faith's father. I noticed that Carl slipped an arm around
Faith's shoulder, or took her hand occasionally, as if to reas-
sure her that she was among friends—that this was simply
another Scovel argument, for general enjoyment.

Tom was already in his old routine of teasing Judy and
Vicki. Blonde head bent toward them, blue eyes fixed upon
them, he was telling one of his gruesome "experiences," not a
word of which was true. "And just as I was about to take the
last step out of the slime, I slipped and . . ." The girls' faces
were alternating revulsion toward the details and pity for
their adored brother, who was delighted that they had not
lost their gullibility.

"How many for coffee?" asked John, coming in from the
kitchen. "How about you, Mom Scovel?"

"Black, please, John," I replied.

He had called me "Mom Scovel." Why had I feared
mother-in-law-hood? On board the *Ryndam,* I had talked to
Fred about it. "I'm scared to death to be a mother-in-law. I'll
say all the wrong things and interfere when I shouldn't. And
I'm sure to give advice."

"You realize all this, so half the battle is won."

"But I won't like having to watch every word I say. It'll
produce a very unnatural, strained atmosphere. I like being
myself."

"Oh, honey, you'll be yourself. Stop worrying." He went
back to reading his book.

"Those poor kids," I murmured, some time later.

"What poor kids?" asked Fred.

"Faith Greeley and John Fitch, our daughter-in-law and
our son-in-law."

"You mean Faith Scovel. I don't feel sorry for them.

They're two very lucky people; they're married to your son and daughter."

"Yours, too. Of course they're lucky, but it'll be hard for them. It isn't like most in-law situations, when you start knowing the other family before you're engaged. We're going to appear after they've been married a matter of years, and they have to accept us as *parents.*"

"It isn't going to be as hard as you think, honey. You'll see."

He had been right, as usual. John gave me the coffee as if he'd been doing it for years. I looked across at Faith, who smiled a beautifully relaxed smile. They were both my children. They even *felt* like my children. These were the two I'd been praying for every day since the birth of Carl and Anne—the children who would grow up to marry them. "I wonder what they look like now?" I had thought at age ten, sixteen, twenty. "I wonder where they are going to school, or where they are working." Now these two of "our other six" had come home, and I felt like singing the doxology.

"Jim, how about you?" I asked, as we drank our coffee.

"I knew you were about to put the screws on your first-born. I saw you watching John and Faith. What do you think of them? Aren't they great?"

"I couldn't have chosen better for Carl and Anne myself. But don't evade the issue."

"Fact is, I can't find a girl who is willing to support me in the manner to which I wish to become accustomed. Or maybe I don't wash my undies in Lux."

"Jim, I'll give you one more year. Then I'm going to use the Oriental method and start looking for a wife for you."

"Do that, Mom. But never mind the time limit. Bring her around when I'm fifty-four and I'll look her over." He rose from the low stool, kissed me and said, "I've got to get to the airport."

Carl and Faith were driving Tom back to his job as counselor at Camp Rabbit Hollow in New Hampshire. Within a few weeks we would be meeting Faith's family at their summer home near there, and Tom would be with us when he was off duty. Fred, Judy, Vicki, and I would leave with Anne and John next morning when they returned to their home in Columbus, New Jersey.

For once, the farewells were happy ones. We were within phoning distance and could drive to see any one of them in a matter of hours. It was as if we had never been away. India and the past had dropped out, as if the pages of my life had been retyped and those experiences deleted. I tried to think of Indian friends and could not recall their faces. Had I lost India forever? That must not be. I would not stop now to think it through. I wanted only to concentrate on how wonderful it was to be home.

~ VIII ~

Driving through New Jersey to Columbus was a dream come true. In China or in India, when difficulties piled too high or when the heat became unbearable, I would "leave" the situation or the weather by the simple method of "changing" the circumstances and the locale. In my mind, I would step into a shining blue car with Fred. We would drive down a smooth highway, windows open to a breeze blown across newly cut hay. Fred would be wearing neatly pressed slacks and a new sport shirt; I, a frock from the pages of *Town and Country*. We were on our way to visit one of our children, of course. We would stop at a Howard Johnson's for lunch and . . .

Except for our being alone in my "escape dream," and except for minor details such as neatly pressed slacks and the *Town and Country* frock, the dream was now coming true. It would be fun to see Anne in her own home, living a grown-up life. What would our child be like as an adult?

But the dream became a nightmare when we reached the New Jersey Turnpike. Never in my life had I traveled at such speed. I was paralyzed with fear. Down a corridor of huge trailer trucks and buses that crisscrossed in front of us from either side, our small car was a prey to the huge vehicles bearing down upon us and hurtling beside us.

"What will I do in this country?" I thought to myself. "I won't be able to get places without a car, but I'll be dead from fright before a month." For almost thirty years, with few exceptions, we had walked wherever we had to go. In India and in China, our "rapid transit" had been by ricksha or bicycle pedicab. Occasional longer journeys were made in the cars of friends who averaged some forty miles an hour—if the rains had not yet begun, or if there were less than the usual number of water buffaloes and oxen on the road. Surely, when we were on furlough in the early 1950's, the average cruising speed of what we then called "autos" was not sixty to seventy miles an hour!

But the traffic thinned out when we reached southern New Jersey. Rich farm land stretched for miles on either side of the turnpike. The sun caught the white of farmhouses and the silver of old barns; the breeze had the freshness of grass. The dream *was* coming true. We even stopped at a Howard Johnson's and ate fried clams, which we had forgotten existed. Waitresses treated us as equals, joked with us in our own language, and seemed glad that we had come. Dishes were clean and sparkling and the ice cream tasted like ice cream, not like the kind that has been made in one's own refrigerator. Later we stopped for a "D.Q." which we learned meant Dairy Queen. It was a new experience in taste and touch—a soft ice cream of just the right consistency. I would have to watch my weight in this country.

In no time at all, we were in Anne's Wedgewood-blue-and-white living room. Antique-white curtains hung at the windows; beloved Grandmother's silver soup tureen reigned in a corner cupboard. First, Anne wanted to show us all that John had made. He was a genius with wood, metals, tools, and electricity.

"He found this washer and dryer in a junkyard in Princeton," said Anne next morning, as I was watching that blessed machine do a pile of clothes it would have taken me all day to wash. Instead, we were going shopping.

"Can't we walk?" I suggested.

"We could, but it's easier to take the car," said Anne. "Then we won't have to carry all the stuff."

People had become centaurs. If you went around the corner to see a neighbor, you drove. Why? Because it took too much time to walk.

Leaving the men at home, we four women went first to the supermarket. What a feeling of power it gave to step up to a door and have it open in front of us! Inside, our eyes were fractured by the bright lights, the bright decorations, the new bright packaging. "Not much like Chora Bazaar," said Vicki. And we thought of the dark, winding street, with its small separate shops for each commodity, its friendly shopkeepers sitting cross-legged within reach of their wares. This sterility, slightly flavored with the smell of paper boxes, cosmetics, and frozen fish, was far different from the robust odor of spices, leather sandals, sweets sizzling in deep fat, perspiration, and incense.

We walked up and down aisles of superabundance, bewildered at how to choose, watching Anne go straight to the article she wanted. Old-time favorite brands of mine had disappeared. In their place were rows of the new detergents, each with a new name and a separate claim. There was an oven cleaner, a chrome cleaner, a leather cleaner, an enamel cleaner, brand after brand of starch, furniture polish, deodorant, cosmetic, and fabric softener. NEW! NEW! NEW! was written on every other package, bottle, or box.

We found a whole aisle of paper things—paper napkins, paper towels, paper hankies, and toilet paper that would really go down when the toilet was flushed! We hadn't been able to afford paper napkins in India, and I had spent hours in China, cutting large sheets of brown paper into toilet-paper size.

To me, the greatest revolution in housekeeping was the all-

purpose rectangular sponge I had found in Anne's kitchen
the night before. How had we ever managed with dishcloths,
I wondered. I bought a dozen of them. "Mother, what are
you going to do with all those sponges?" asked Anne. I had
forgotten for the moment that I did not have to lay in a
supply for a year. I could come back tomorrow and buy more,
or wait a week. I could buy anything I wanted to buy, any
time I wanted to buy it!

And the food! Oh, the food! Pepperidge Farm bread that
we had talked about nostalgically. Olives—ripe or green,
large or small, pitted or unpitted! *Olives!* And cheese! There
was no such thing as food in season. One did not have to eat
umpteen varieties of squash because that was all that could
be grown in the summer months. If you wanted asparagus,
you ate asparagus. If you craved strawberries, you ate strawberries. The frozen foods were a miracle.

"When I was little I used to think alphabet soup was the
greatest thing outside of scotch tape in the world," said Judy,
standing before the shelves of canned goods. She read us off
the names of soups we'd never heard of.

Buying clothes was completely confusing. Racks of dresses
in strange colors were switched before us, but which were the
styles we should choose and which only the fad of the moment? We could only know by asking Anne. When we put
on our little fashion show for the men after dinner, we felt
she had chosen well.

The men had spent the day buying a car. Fred had been
able to get a 1956 Chevrolet from the Marvin Nelsons, who
had been on furlough and were leaving next day for India.
Imagine owning a car!

"Are you going to have M.D. on your license plates?"
Anne asked her father.

"I don't know, I hadn't thought about it," he replied.
"Maybe I'd better. With all these accidents I hear about,

people might need to stop me some time."

"If anyone but a state trooper stops you at the scene of an accident, step on the gas and go on," said John.

It did not sound like John. "I know you're thinking 'What about the Good Samaritan?' But you have to be careful these days. There has been case after case of doctors stopping to help and being sued later by the accident victim or his family. And the cases are won, at that."

"But suppose *you* have an accident," I said. "How do you get help, John?"

"If you are on a main highway, the police will find you eventually. There are still good Joes left in the world, but you can't count on it any more. The papers are full of stories of violence where those witnessing the deed don't interfere or even call for help."

"Why?" we all asked at once.

"Nobody wants to get involved. It takes time. People are too busy to take time to go to court, or even to pick someone up and take him to the hospital—especially when they may get sued for it later."

I thought of the prayer I had prayed so glibly in my childhood, "From battle and murder and from sudden death, good Lord, deliver us." Now it meant *us*.

"If people are too busy to care, we are catapulting downhill at terrific speed," I said.

"Let's change the subject," said Anne. She refilled the coffee cups and passed out pieces of her delicious homemade pound cake. "Daddy, how do you like Vicki's new hair style?"

"All four of you look very modern," said Fred, "but I sure do miss Vicki's ponytail."

"Daddy, are you sorry I did it?" asked Vicki. "I really didn't want to have it cut off, because you liked it, but Anne made me, didn't you, Anne?"

"Yes, I certainly did."

"Okay, honey," Fred said to Vicki. "We have to bring you up to the times, I suppose. All of you look gorgeous."

"Of course they do," said Anne. "I'm giving Judy and Vicki Bobbi curls tomorrow."

"What are Bobbi curls?" asked Judy.

There was so much to learn.

"I think I'll take a bath and go to bed," I said, stretching.

"You had a bath this morning," said Fred.

"I can't get over the luxury of being able to turn on a faucet and have all the hot water you want filling the tub. Then, to pick up a cake of fragrant soap and lather yourself freely, knowing that when that cake is gone you can buy another at the supermarket . . ."

"You always were a capitalist at heart," said Fred.

"What did you do for baths in India?" asked John.

"Go ahead with your luxuries. I'll tell him," said Fred. I knew every word he would be saying.

"First, you remember to tell the cook enough hours ahead so he can heat the *hamam*."

"What's a *hamam*?"

"It's a large tin cylinder on legs—a drum with a place in the center for a charcoal fire. Ours usually leaked, and Chandru would plaster the holes with gobs of bread dough. If you were the only one to have a bath, you got two pails of hot water; otherwise only one, always with cinders and small pieces of bread dough floating in it. Meanwhile, you've dragged the tin tub to the part of the cement floor in the bathroom where the drain is located, so you can empty it easily afterward. The tub is four feet long and two feet wide. John, did you ever try curling up in a tub that size?"

John admitted he hadn't.

"Your knees are level with your eyes, and every slosh depletes the water that much more. In fact, two pails of hot water are really more than the tub can hold with you in it. You soap yourself carefully, because there isn't enough water to rinse yourself thoroughly. In winter, when the oil stove only heats one corner of the room, you're in and out as quickly as possible. But in summer you can finish up with water from the faucet. It will be hot, even too hot, because the pipes run along the roof in the sun. You can have an icy shower any day you want it, in winter."

"Don't they have plumbing in India?"

"Of course they do. You should see the efficient new apartments in Ludhiana and the magnificent hotels in New Delhi. I'm talking about the hundred-year-old mud-brick mission houses *we* lived in. And we had plumbing, too, of a sort."

When Fred came to bed, I was still "luxuriating." "Get out of that tub," he called. "You've got a big day tomorrow. Remember?"

We were leaving Judy and Vicki at Anne's (with a pile of comics) and were driving north to Thiels, New York, to spend the day with my brother's family. We were going to look for a house.

~ IX ~

"Damn all missionaries," said my brother, as we sat in the Scott's living room that evening.

"Bob!" said his wife, Dorothy.

"Why—this time?" I asked, unperturbed.

"They haven't got a grain of sense," he replied, squirming in his leather chair. "I've lived here thirteen years and I haven't bought a house yet."

"You don't have to when you live in a lovely old white one on the bank of a stream," I said. "You have a home."

"I know, but you two have only been in town one day. *One day,* and you've already given away fifty of your scant dollars for an option on a place you've only looked at once."

"Well, it's the one we want," I told him.

"How do you know? You've only looked at four."

"Six. We looked at two in Pearl River on our way here. One was impossibly dingy and the other a beautiful Victorian gimcracky one . . ."

"Which would take a fortune to heat and another fortune to make livable," said Fred.

"I'm glad somebody in this family has some sense," said Bob.

Dorothy was getting nervous about a possible family flare-up. "Now, Bob, you mustn't talk to your sister that way," she

55

said, leaning across to lay a hand on his arm.

"She wouldn't know she was home if I didn't," her husband replied.

"You should have heard us when we were children," I said. "I don't know how Mother ever stood us."

"You never did have a brain in your head," said Bob.

I was home, with a real, honest, frank, teasing *relative*. How I loved him!

"Now I'm just going to drive you past a few places," Bob had said that morning, "so you'll get an idea of the kind of place you can buy for the amount of money you have to spend. You aren't going to go inside a single house. That will come later. It takes time to decide on the house you'll probably be living in the rest of your life. We'll start with Stony Point and then look at other places in the county."

"No other town feels right," I said.

"That has nothing to do with it," said Bob emphatically. "Fred, how *do* you manage to live with her?"

"Patience, long-suffering, and an extremely kind and affectionate disposition," he replied.

"To quote an old Scovel saying, 'That remark will be treated with the silence it so richly deserves.' " I told them.

The first three houses had no character. But the fourth was nestled in a soft, green hill overlooking the Hudson River—the river beside which I had been born and brought up. The house had a gray stone front, white aluminum siding, and rambler roses over the doorway. Bob, who had driven by very slowly, stepped on the gas. "Please, *please* may we go in?" I begged.

"Yes, Bob, can't we take a look at this one?" asked Fred.

"Okay, but don't make up your minds on anything."

"Come right in," said the Paesanis, an Italian family who proceeded to show us the house. I knew at once that this was

to be our home. And I saw it, not as it was, but as it would
be. The porch along the side of the house could be divided
into an entrance hall and Fred's study. We would enlarge the
living room by including the kitchen, so that the room
would extend the full length of the house. The dining room,
on the other side of the house, would become the new
kitchen. With only three of us at home most of the time, we
could easily manage by eating at one end of the kitchen or
living room.

Grandmother's heavy mahogany furniture would need
lighter walls than the present dark green and maroon. The
Paesanis would be taking with them, of course, the uphol-
stered furniture, the large white and gold lamps (I was intrigued by their bases of graceful ballet dancers doing the
split), and the large TV set. We were *not* going to have a
television set. I had already seen enough of conversation
monopolized by the mechanical voices of people I preferred
not to hear.

Best of all, the house was expandable. The basement room,
now half finished with wood paneling, would be Tom's
room. Later, when the marrieds and their families arrived,
we could easily put up a double bed, a single bed, and even a
crib when that became necessary. Judy would have the main-
floor bedroom and half bath, Vicki one of the two upstairs
bedrooms and we the other.

"How could anyone build a house with clothes closets
along the river side?" I asked Mrs. Paesani.

"I'm sure I'll never know," she replied. "We were always
going to have dormers put in."

"Just the thing," I said. "A dormer with three windows
will be my study. I always write in the bedroom anyway.
We'll have bookcases set into the side walls." I could picture
the typewriting table before the window, with an even
better view of the river than the one from the living room
below.

Fred and Bob were talking in low whispers. "How about this house?" Fred asked.

"It's within your price range," Bob answered.

"We just can't let this get away," I said as we walked back to the car. "We've *got* to have it. What do we do now?"

"Well, you can put a down payment on it to hold it," said Bob. "Remember, this doesn't mean you're going to take it. Pay the money down, if you must, then forget the whole business and start looking around. You two mustn't decide on anything for at least three months. And whatever you decide on will have to cost under eighteen thousand. That certainly narrows your choice, so look carefully."

What Bob did not realize was the urgency of finding a house and finding it quickly. This had to be more than a temporary place to live. It must be a base of security for two girls in a strange country, who had all their lives moved into each new house with the certainty that they must soon leave it.

We had tried to make these houses into homes and to make them seem permanent. For this reason, wherever we went, we unpacked quickly and completely. And we never changed the decor. Fred and I had moving down to a science. Boxes and suitcases were packed with living room things on top, including curtains, rugs, pictures, and bric-a-brac. By night of the first day, we would have one room completely furnished and could have a meal beside the fire or before an open window looking out upon what would be a garden.

Even the pictures would be hung—the snow scene over the mantel, where it had hung in beloved Grandmother's home. Wrought-iron candlesticks (early Scovels had brought them from England) took their accustomed place, one on either side of "Aunt Martha," the family clock. Across from my low rocker sat Fred's chair, its wide arms furnishing good seats for those wanting a bedtime story. The smallest of a nest of Chinese tables, within easy reach of the armchair, held a pipe and the battered bronze ash tray that Fred refused to give up. His father's name, "Carl Scovel," was embossed upon it (and, incidentally, "Rotary International"). A narrow table broke the longest wall space. Over it hung the landscape done by the Chinese artist whom Fred had invited to give demonstrations to his medical staff, in order to interest them in the fine arts. The couch took up the end of the room opposite the fireplace. The scene never varied. If we moved in June, the children knew exactly where the Christmas crèche would be set up next December.

But we fooled no one, least of all ourselves. We all knew we must pack up and move again. This was different. We had had many homes in various places in the world. This would be the first time we had owned a house to put one in. I hoped it would see us through until the rest of the children were married and in their own homes.

At any rate, we had no time to waste on a temporary place. Tom must have a home to come to between camp and college. We must let Judy feel that she had a base before she left for her college in less than two months. Vicki would attend high school in the next town and should acquire something of a settled feeling before having to adjust to a working mother. The three older children must be given the home they had not had since childhood.

Or was I only rationalizing my own strong desire to be unpacked and have everything under one roof for the first time in my thirty years of married life? Time pressed upon me from every direction and gave me no way out. It was already July 25, and there was still the work to be done on the interior of the house.

"If you had plenty of time, would you still want this house?" asked Fred.

I thought for only a moment. "I certainly would."

"I hoped you would say that."

Bob was willing to be pushed, though he warned us that we might regret not having looked further. Four days later, we signed the contract with the Paesanis, the papers to be held in escrow until we could get permission to remodel the house. We had an Irish lawyer, the Paesanis an Italian one. The real-estate broker was Dutch; the "referee" a Jewish rabbi. It was just the kind of a start we needed for our home-to-be.

On the way back to Anne and John's, Fred said, "Let's celebrate. Let's stop at the next Howard Johnson's and have dinner alone. How long has it been since you and I have sat down together alone?"

"Aeons of centuries," I said. "We'll phone the kids and tell them not to wait. Think of it, Fred, we've bought a home, our own home."

"We've bought the front-door knob. I don't know how long it will be before the rest of the house really belongs to us, but we've made the right beginning."

"And that doorknob is an antique, I want you to know. Did you notice the lovely old brass, worn satiny by the hands of three or four generations? I don't know how it came to be on an eight-year-old house. This is the first time we've ever owned a doorknob with a house attached to it."

We talked of nothing but the house all through our meal. Over coffee, Fred said, "I still don't see how you could go into that house and see the possibilities you saw."

"Remember my verse from Exodus?" I said, " 'Behold, I send an angel before thee to keep thee in the way and to bring thee to the place which I have prepared.' From the moment I saw it, I felt as if this were the place prepared.' "

"I have a feeling we won't be sorry we did what we did," said Fred. "We can start out tomorrow on our round of family reunions with something to come back to."

X

The first stop in our family tour was at the home of my sister, Geneva, and her big-hearted, red-headed Irishman husband, whom we all loved. They lived in our old home town, Mechanicville, New York. Geneva and I had had our families at the same time, joking about running neck and neck, as the fourth, fifth, and sixth children were born. But Geneva had won the race by two children.

"Six or eight, not much difference," said Leonard. "That's what we get for marrying the Scott girls, Fred."

"You still have the slim, lithe figure of a teen-ager," I said to Geneva. "I'm jealous."

"You should be." She smiled. "I've beaten you at grandchildren, too. We have eight."

It would take us a little time to sort out the married names of the children, and to remember which grandchild belonged to which family. "I even have trouble sometimes myself," said Leonard. Judy and Vicki were delighted to meet a new crop of cousins.

We went on to the new, modern apartment of my youngest sister, Helen Moore. It was here that I realized for the first time that I would never see my mother and father again. They had died while we were in India, and the miles separating us had somehow kept away the finality of death. Only the beloved memories had come flooding in. Now I knew my childhood home was gone. And Fred did not even have a brother or a sister to visit. How very precious the house in Stony Point seemed now.

"One reason I married this wife of mine was to become part of a large family, and especially to get such a good-looking sister-in-law," Fred said to Helen. She was preparing a huge steak for the evening meal. "Flattery will get you nowhere," said Helen, "but keep it up; I love it.

"We'll eat in the kitchen. I'll fix trays for the girls in the living room."

"But they haven't been away from that television long enough to say two words to you," I remonstrated. "Look at them."

Through the kitchen doorway, the three of us watched them, sitting on the floor, legs crossed, bodies forward, hypnotized by the rectangle of moving light and shadow.

"Leave them alone," said Helen. "They'll soon tire of it."

"I hope so."

"Mind if I watch the news with them?" asked Fred.

"Not you, too!" I said.

Back at the kitchen table, Helen looked at me. "Myra, you're going to have to accept things here."

"I know it; I *do* know it. It's just that I can't help looking at things with the eyes of a foreigner. Those corny jingles, women you don't even know taking baths in your living room. I can't get used to it. And the comedians. Though I ache from laughing at them, I keep looking around to see if there are any Chinese or Indians present who might resent some reference to their country or 'get' an off-color joke."

"You're not in India or China; you're here," said Helen, "and I get the idea that you wish you weren't—that you don't like America very much."

"Helen, how can you say that!" I was aghast. "I love America, perhaps more than you do, because I know what a wonderful country America is. You who are here all the time have no idea what rolling hills and opulent cows really mean; or rich fields and beautiful roads stretching out over the country. You look at them, but you don't see them, because you haven't seen cracked, parched fields, starving people, and the complete lack of farm animals. I'm glad you haven't. I'm glad there's still a place in the world where nobody knows what starvation is, but . . ."

"Okay, okay. You don't have to give me your missionary speech," she said, smiling. "I just don't want you to go gallivanting off again because you're not satisfied here."

I thought a lot about what Helen had said as we drove on to see Carl and Faith in New Hampshire. I, too, had always taken it for granted that America was the best country in the world and that all men, everywhere, could only admit that this was true. Then I found out that every country has its own unique contribution to make. We met people, a very special kind of people, who had much to teach us. We were confronted by an ancient heritage and a culture that seeped into individuals and took from them the restlessness found in our young country. They, too, surprisingly, thought theirs was the best country in the world. They were not at all impressed by size or strength or mounting statistics.

"But America isn't just steel and concrete structures piercing the sky," I wanted to shout. "It isn't a continual sex movie or a wild West show or a huge diplomat towering over you. America is people—people you'd like, people who care what happens to you."

But the trouble was that when you had been away from your country for years, you began to believe that every fellow American was like the people you loved and admired most. You had only to board a ship before disillusionment began to set in. And as you floundered like a fish on hot sand, you knew that you, too, had changed. You were no longer impressed by size or strength or mounting statistics. You were looking for that something else you'd been so sure of overseas, when you spoke to others about America.

You had to search for it when you got back home, but you found it. Wonderful things were happening—new art, new poetry, the Peace Corps, the Negro standing like a man, war no longer considered the chivalrous way to settle differences. You saw, too, the great potential of your country. Men were free to do what they wanted to do, free to create, with all the tools and materials in their hands, but they did not see what they were holding. You wanted to cry. All it would take to make the world the Kingdom of God on earth was lying there in men's hands, and they could not feel the weight of it on their palms.

"Where do I, as an individual, begin?" I wondered.

"You have to accept America," Helen had said. "You are not in India or China, you are here." How I loved being here, driving through these New England villages with their atmosphere of perpetual Sunday afternoon. Accept America? I wanted to put my arms around it and give it one big hug.

Rounding a corner of a village green, we were smacked in the eyes by the sign on a church lawn:

> Fun and Frolic
> tonight at 8
> IMMACULATE CONCEPTION

We were not in India. I said it to myself again. But, my dear Father, God, what must You think of a sign like this one? How could I explain *this* to an Indian friend? I wanted to stop to explain to the priest that the sign must be taken down.

❧ XI ❧

"There's one sharp corner on this hearth that needs to be filed down or rounded," I said to Fred one morning as we were working on our new house.

"No hurry about that," he said. "I'll get around to it after I get the kitchen floor done."

"Well, I don't know . . ."

"Don't worry, honey, your grandchild isn't even born yet. He won't be able to get himself around that corner for another year at least."

"*Our* grandchild, and maybe it's a she. I get so excited I can hardly wait."

"I guess you'll have to," he said, as he went out to lay the kitchen linoleum.

"I don't see how you can be so calm about it," I called after him. "This baby will be our very first grandchild."

"A baby is a baby," he called back. "I'll get excited when I can take him . . .

"Or her."

"Or her—on a hike."

The announcement had been made when the Scovels and the Greeleys had gathered on the grass outside the old New Hampshire farmhouse where the family spent its summers. We were there to celebrate our reunion and Faith's sister Cindy's birthday. I had been looking across the lower hills to

Mt. Monadnock and thinking that the air in our country had a different smell than in any other place on earth. I was brought back by Carl's call for silence and an announcement that Cindy had a birthday card to read to us all. With a shake of her long brown hair, she took her place beside Carl, began to read, then screamed. Between her excited gasps, we learned that she was to be an aunt the following February.

Faith hurried across to me. "I didn't tell you when we met you in New York because I knew how very much Anne had wanted to meet you at the ship with your first grandchild, and I didn't want to bring any unhappiness to her that day."

"What a lucky man Carl is to have such a thoughtful wife," I said, thinking, too, of how careful she had been not to detract from her sister's birthday.

The blessed news seemed the very culmination of all anyone could possibly ask as a home-coming—a grandchild, and we were here to hold the baby in our arms! Life was so perfect it was almost frightening.

"I've learned one thing about these do-it-yourself products," Fred called from the kitchen, "whenever the instructions say 'All you have to do is just . . . ,' you're in for trouble. What are *you* doing?"

"Scraping a few more layers of this slime-colored varnish off what will one day be the gleaming white woodwork of your study," I told him. I wasn't as optimistic of the outcome as I sounded. Perspiration poured down my face, the paint remover stung, the wire brush missed the woodwork and skinned a thumb. "All you have to do is just . . ."

"I need a cup of coffee badly," I called to Fred. "Can I still get to the stove?"

"I left a path for that very purpose," he called back. "Come out and see how you like your new kitchen floor."

"Those squares look much better than they did in the

store. Must be your magic touch. Do you want a Fig New-
ton?"

We sat at the table looking across at one another. "I still
can't believe we're here," said Fred.

"Are you sure that Stony Point is the place *you* wanted to
be, or did I push you into it?" I asked, watching him closely.

"Of all the ridiculous ideas! Of course you didn't push me
into coming here. We've always talked of coming here. Remember when we almost bought a lot on Crickettown Road
before we went to India?"

We had arrived in Stony Point the first time in the Spring
of 1951, after our release from Communist China. We lived
then in a renovated old Dutch farmhouse on the thirty-acre
Gilmor-Sloane estate. Four Gilmor sisters had left their beautiful home and this old farmhouse to the then Board of
Foreign Missions of the Presbyterian Church in the U.S.A.
Conferences and retreats were held at the *big* house, as we
always called it. We lived in one half of the farmhouse, which
had been made into two apartments for missionaries on furlough. Our spirits had been badly beaten by the harassment
of living under Communism, and I had taken it harder than
Fred. I was in need of healing and there was something thera-
peutic about the stolid stone walls which had squatted between the same fields for generations and the perfect arc of
bird flight against a ballet of dogwoods in full bloom.

The friends we made in the community and in that bulwark of gray stone, the Stony Point Presbyterian Church,
were healing people. Edna and Ernie Moser, host and hostess
of the Gilmor-Sloane estate, were two of the best people on
earth and one reason why we had chosen to live here. The
community was made up of people who helped with no idea
they were helping; they were simply being their own whole-
some selves.

It had taken a few months of living where I could see the

sky from every window before I could fully comprehend that we were free. Later, I could recall the day, the hour, and the spot in the bedroom where I had stood when it suddenly came to me that no matter where I went in this glorious country, my suitcase would never be opened for inspection. I could travel anywhere I wanted to, cross any state border without a permit. When I packed for an overnight speaking trip, I could do so without having to look at each article to see whether it would cause suspicion. I could tuck in a notebook, a letter, a book without thinking it might be used as evidence against me. And I could speak in public without weighing each word to see how it would sound played back on a tape recorder. We could have coffee with a friend, knowing that he had not risked his life to get in to see us. We could take long walks in the woods, down to the river, *anywhere,* without being followed to see if we were trying to escape. We could take that walk knowing that we *had* escaped.

" 'Deliverance' is a wonderful word," I said to Fred, as we sat at the kitchen table. "We don't begin to deserve all that we have been given."

"Nobody could deserve what *we've* got." He tamped the tobacco down in his pipe, lit it, and drank the last gulp of coffee. "We'd better get back to work." But he made no move.

"I know where I'd like to hang the children's work sheet," I said.

"Where?"

"There." I showed him the spot between the stove and the sink. "Right where we will see it every time we let the hot water run or take a cold drink or prepare a good meal."

When the children were growing up, we tried to vary their household chores so they wouldn't "get stuck with the same

jobs forever." I made out a new list every week—Jim, dishes
at noon; Carl, sweep porches; Anne, dishes at night, and so
forth. The plan had continued in the concentration camp
where the chores were heavier.

One day, an artist who was interned with us, Daisy Atter-
bury, came into the courtyard as I was leaning on a stone
drawing off the lines for a new work sheet. "Let me do this
one," she said. She took out her watercolors and drew the
little round faces of each child above the work columns.
Then she used the children's initials instead of their names,
as she listed what each would be doing—profiles for J and C,
fullface for A, drawing in the expression she expected Jim,
Carl, or Anne might have as they faced a particular chore—
broad grins for taking Tom to school, tired frowns for carrying heavy pails of water, disgust at emptying the garbage.
Unpacking after the Sino-Japanese War, we found that work
sheet, folded in an apron pocket, and had it framed at
once.

"I'll hang it right now," said Fred. "Then it will be done."

"Do you think we should have a plaque on it saying something like, 'This family must never forget that it has had two
miracles of deliverance—one from a Japanese concentration
camp and one from the Communists'?" I asked.

"It wouldn't mean much to anyone unless they had experienced it," said Fred. "This is kind of a private family remembrance."

~~ XII ~~

"Isn't today Tuesday?" I asked Fred one day a few weeks later.

"Yep," he replied.

"The washing machine was supposed to be delivered yesterday."

"Maybe they phoned while we were at the Post Office. We weren't away long enough to have missed them if they had come."

We had taken a loan from the bank to buy the washer and a refrigerator.

"You'd better establish your credit rating as soon as possible," my brother Bob told us. I could not understand why the only way you could establish your credit rating was by owing money.

"You'd better get a dryer, too, while you're at it," he said.

"What on earth do I want a dryer for?" I asked. "My clothes would never get the sun and the wind through them. And besides, we'd owe that much more money. I can't bear being in debt and Fred doesn't like it any better than I do."

"That's the way people buy things these days," said Bob.

So many changes had taken place, or had distance and the years made us idealize America and Americans? Now we had to owe money in order to be considered respectable. It was a far cry from my father's agony over the few dollars he owed.

And why did people say, even promise, that they would do something and then not do it? We had accepted the Oriental total disregard of time—what difference did it make whether the thing arrived on Monday or Friday? But the salesmen here could be so convincing when they said, "We'll deliver it on Monday. You're sure you will be home?"

"Morning or afternoon?" we'd ask.

"Morning. Between ten and eleven."

"Why can't they say right out, 'We'll get it up there some-time within the next two weeks, depending on when the truck is free,' " said Fred. "I don't understand it. I should think it would be poor business—bad public relations."

We soon learned that the public expected such treatment. "How'd you ever get it so soon?" asked a neighbor, when the washer arrived two weeks later. It was *not* on a Monday, and it was not between ten and eleven in the morning.

We had more to learn.

"Now, Lady," said the comedian who also understood the installation of washing machines, "You see this here filter? You understand how to clean it? 'Cause if you don't, you're gonna have a flood in this here cellar. Boy! Are you gonna have a flood! If you're plannin' on a basement swimming pool, just go ahead and let this thing clog up." Once more, he showed me how to clean the filter.

"I never swim in wash water," I assured him. "I chose this machine because it had a filter I could clean."

"Well, this one'll give you good service then. Should last you five years or more," he said as if he had just presented me with the queen of all washers.

"Five years?" I said. "Surely you mean fifteen."

"You gotta be kiddin'."

"But this has to last the rest of my life!"

"Oh, you're going to live longer than that—a pretty little woman like you."

"My mother had the same washing machine for as long as I could remember."

"They don't make 'em like that any more. Haven't you ever heard of built-in obsolescence?"

We hadn't. Neither Fred nor I could believe that a company would actually build a machine, a car, *anything*, with the express purpose of having something go wrong with it within a given period of time. All our lives in China, we had been hearing the Chinese say, "This is a good tool. You can depend on it. I've had it for years and it still works as well as ever. It's American."

The last few years in India, we had been hearing, "That's no good; it's American. You'd better buy a Japanese one." We had put it down to anti-American feeling following our government's aid to Pakistan, but perhaps the Indians had learned of built-in obsolescence from experience. We refused to believe it. American know-how and American integrity had always gone hand in hand. How had this rumor started?

The concept was far more frightening to us than it could possibly have been to the jovial man who had just finished installing our washing machine. We had seen China fall, not so much because of diplomatic policies in high places or poor military preparation, as because of the loss of integrity of individual people—one Chinese private stealing a few guns and selling them to the Communists; another, seeing the profits, getting into the business; then everyone out to make his wad. Was it happening here? Didn't people realize that democracy was built on the integrity of the individual? Surely Americans were not naïve enough to think, "Oh, it doesn't matter what *I* do." Our countrymen had certainly outgrown that adolescent attitude, or we were in for the holocaust so many seemed to fear.

"Calm down, honey," said Fred. "It can't be that bad. Got any dirty clothes? Let's try out the new washer."

The refrigerator arrived; the paint came; the mailbox was up, the garbage can bought, the grass mowed. The furniture stored in Rochester or kept for us by friends was delivered. We had a bad moment when we realized that Grandmother's huge mahogany bed could not be maneuvered up the narrow stairway. Luckily, the upstairs dormer had not been put in, and the mover managed to swing up the bed pieces on ropes and push them through the opening in the side of the house.

"Wait until one of our children wants to move it out of here some day," said Fred. "The legend will arise that the bed was built right here in this room."

Not a week went by without a familiar car swinging into the driveway—one or more of the children arriving to help. Each of them wanted to have a part in establishing their home. Jim took his vacation from the Elmira, New York, *Star Gazette* to put in larger-paned windows on the river side of the living room. He spent hours working out the puzzle of how best it could be done. Carl scraped woodwork and painted, after having first run up the flag in the front yard "to show that the king is in residence."

Vicki baby-sat evenings so a friend of ours (whose wife worked nights) could help with the heavy carpentry and give Fred instructions as the work went along. Vicki also painted the walls and woodwork of her own room. I insisted that Faith keep away from the painting. An old wives' tale, perhaps, but experience corroborated that the smell of paint was not good for a woman expecting a baby.

Suddenly there was one more darling who could not paint! Anne and John phoned their good news. They were coming to see the fun and to share the happiness of the expectation of their first child. Not to be counted out of the family work party, Anne made our India print into curtains for the kitchen while we talked of Brother Li and the Rose Sisters and about prayer and miracles.

After cutting back the strangling vines from the hedges and getting most of the meals, Judy managed to get some new clothes made for college. She would be leaving for Western College in Oxford, Ohio, in a matter of days. Tom got home from camp in time to buy for us and nail over the front door the wrought-iron numerals, 37. Now we had an address. We finished his mounds of laundry in the new machine and he was off to Wooster College, in Ohio, for another year. We had hardly seen him. But, he would be home for Christmas; so would Judy, so would they all!

Gradually the house became home. The woodwork was white; the walls were soft rose-cream, a color we had found in the interior of the Bulfinch church in Peterborough, New Hampshire. It made the perfect background for the mahogany furniture, which looked less battered from its many trips around the world, now that it had been rubbed down with the new spray polishes. The blue Chinese rug, made by the Fetti Company of Peking according to Mother Scovel's specifications, was like new, having been properly cleaned and mended by experts. The tapestry of the venerable Chinese scholar at his mountain retreat, which we had bought from an equally venerable Chinese gentleman in Tsining, Shantung, now hung over our bed as it had hung over the iron bed in the concentration camp. "Our culture corner" we had called it.

"Aunt Martha," the family clock, at rest on a shelf above the hearth, was a conversation piece:

"Notice this scene, 'View in Italy,' painted on the glass," we would begin. "That lower half of the clock was broken when Mother Scovel's household possessions arrived in China. She called in the local carpenter, Chu Lao San, and asked him to mend it with brass brads, as the Chinese mend porcelain. When Lao San returned the clock, Mother looked it over carefully. 'Why there isn't even a sign of a crack!' she exclaimed. 'How did you ever do it so perfectly?'

" 'I couldn't fix it,' replied Lao San, 'so I took a new piece of glass and painted another picture.' It is an exact duplicate, even to the broken letters in the title."

Having lost two complete households of furniture (including all our books and records), one to the Japanese army and one to the Communists, we thought we knew better than to become attached to material possessions. Life, limb, and sanity had loomed so much more important in the circumstances under which our household "gods" had been lost. As Judy said, "If your life is at stake, nothing is more important than that. But if everything is going along smoothly, other things become important. Maybe that's why it is so much easier to get attached to material things here in the States than in another country where they are only temporary aids to living."

I was certainly glad that we had been allowed to ship Mother Scovel's things to America after she died in Canton, though at the time it mattered little whether or not I ever saw them again. The last crate went out only a few days before the Communists took the city.

"God must have wanted us to have them in our new house," I said to Fred as we were unpacking. It was good to have "Aunt Martha" comfortably ticking the hours away in a home of her own. And I found that certain things were endowed with a special grace given them by loving people— the lace doily, for instance, mended so perfectly by Mother Philomena, who had been dying of tuberculosis when she was brought into our hospital in Ludhiana. Where was she now? Still in her convent in India, perhaps. I spread the delicate white lace on the shining surface of the Scovel claw-footed table. Upon it sat the blue pitcher belonging to my mother's wedding set of dishes. Only her generosity had made it possible for me to own that pitcher now.

En route for one of our furloughs from China, we had stopped in Los Angeles to visit my father's sister. One day she took out the blue pitcher, saying, "The first time I ever visited in your home, right after your father and mother were married, I admired this pitcher. It was part of your mother's set of dishes. She helped me pack to go home, and when I opened the trunk, there was the pitcher hidden among the clothes. Here, I want you to have it."

"But Aunt Nell, it's yours," I said. "Mother wanted you to have it."

"I have enjoyed it all these years. I never got over your mother's breaking her set of wedding china to give me the pitcher I liked so much. Your mother was like that, Myra. And now this really belongs to you."

I used it for daffodils. Mother had loved the spring flowers.

There was another pitcher which we unpacked, a small silver one, just right for violets and lilies-of-the-valley. It had been given to us by our assigned "family" of medical students at the Christian Medical College in Ludhiana, and it was inscribed, "To Dr. and Mrs. Scovel, 1953-59, with love from Group D." "We wanted to write, 'To *Mamaji* and *Papaji*,' one of the students told us, but some thought it was not appropriate for engraving on silver."

We knew we were completely settled when the neighborhood children began to drop in frequently. Nicki and Butch and Bruce and the Jones boys were the first to call. They would gather around the piano as Nicki led them in singing. He could start them off with "and a one, and a two, and a three," like the TV star, Lawrence Welk. The Dacre children who lived next door were out of the house to help, back door banging, if Fred so much as lifted a hoe.

As soon as all the leaves were off the trees that first Autumn, we discovered we were living at the center of a wide curve in the Hudson, the bay between Grassy Point and Stony Point. Without knowing it, we had come home to "River Bend," the fictitious name I had chosen for Stony Point in my first writing.

Now that all dreams had come true, what would life be like? Would it have meaning, now that one no longer had to come to grips with basic things like hunger and prayer?

XIII

There had been days on end when we had prayed, "Give us this day our daily bread," knowing that if God did not answer our prayer, we would not eat. There had been times when we had prayed, "Deliver us from evil" in the certainty that only He could keep us from becoming the victims of an emotion-starved victorious army. We had experienced the miracle of deliverance, and we had seen firsthand the suffering of those who deserved to be spared as much as, or more than, we and yet were not spared. Why? The question continually stabbed us.

Here, it was a relief not to question, not to have to pray for deliverance. Little prayers of thanksgiving were on our lips for new and surprising blessings at every turn. Lilacs, forsythia, lilies-of-the-valley, violets, and daffodils were the flowers we had always wanted in our garden; they had all been planted for us. We were thankful for the familiar, "just right" look of things. Nothing was "foreign"; the trees were our trees; the river, our river. Prayers of thanks were inevitable, but not the striving prayers of intercession. I did not want them back—at least, not yet.

And I was tired of feeling guilty for having what those around me did not have. We had never become accustomed to the poverty we saw. Here, everyone we met had as much or more than we, and I had no desire to seek out those who had less. I wanted to *enjoy* America—to close the door on the world and its troubles, to prolong the bliss of having no reason to clutch at God and not let Him go.

This was part of my resentment against television, I decided. It wasn't only the demonstrations of how to hold your false teeth in your mouth; it was the sight of violence going on, and dope being peddled in the lilac-scented town in which you lived.

I wanted to forget violence for as long as I lived. But on our first Fourth of July in America we had to relive the hell of bombings with every giant firecracker that went off. And though firecrackers were against the law here, the explosions continued around us until the early morning hours. It seemed a strange way to celebrate the birth of our country's freedom.

On all the other days, except perhaps when a truck backfired, we lived as on the calm surface of a lake, and gradually I realized that this was only a surface life. I had to get my roots into the *ground* of America, to feel those roots grapple the stones of the present situation here.

"Paul knew 'both how to be abased and how to abound,' " I quoted to Fred, as we were driving to the supermarket one evening. "I don't know how to abound."

"Are you going to be like the old monks who thought there was virtue in wearing a hair shirt?" he asked.

"You feel so *good* in a hair shirt—virtuous, I mean. It's so much easier to be a good Christian in 'hunger and want' than it is in 'plenty and abundance,' because when you're really in want, you have no place to go but to God."

"And you think you can manage alone in plenty?" he asked.

Suddenly I realized the dangers of the abundant life. You made all your own decisions. You drifted into following the "devices" (they could be so devious) and the "desires of your own heart." This was what was meant by the "wide, easy road that leads to destruction." Among all the many broad highways opening before me now, how could I find the particular narrow path that God had ordained for me to walk in?

I thought of those who had lost their way—the doctor who might have found the cure for cancer, but who had chosen what by now had become a successful, boring practice; the man who had held the reins of world peace in his hands and dropped them because he feared the next election; the woman who had held her husband back from solving the problems of thousands of refugees. How much harm had I done already?

Choices. Every day we were going to be faced with a wealth of choices we had not had before. We couldn't go back to "the simple life," and we certainly couldn't go forward alone into the complexity of this kind of a future. Because of the very multitude of choices, we were more dependent upon God than ever before.

"I'm going to get up an hour earlier. It's my only way out," I told Fred. "I've got to have some time for prayer and for at least a little Bible study."

"Good idea," he said, as he slid the car into the parking lot. He was out of the car before he fully realized what I had said. "But that will be six A.M. on the days we're commuting to the office. You'll need your beauty sleep."

"That's why *you* keep so steady spiritually," I said "—all that time on your knees. I don't see how you can kneel that long. All I'd be thinking about would be how uncomfortable I was."

"Ridiculous," he murmured as he reached into the back seat for the empty Coke bottles. "Are you going to sit there and philosophize all night, or are we going to get some shopping done?"

It was good to see the sunrise again. It was good to be alone with God. I was home, at last.

And we bought our first television set. Actually, Vicki and Fred bought the set and presented it to me *after* they had installed it in the basement room. "I had to, Mother," Vicki explained. "So many of my assignments at school take for granted that I've seen things on television."

Fred grinned like a schoolboy caught in the act. They need not have worried. I was ready for television now that I had fully accepted my role as a present-day American. I surrendered to the charms of Danny Kaye, Garry Moore, the Miss America contest (which Vicki and I enjoyed together), the Bell Telephone Hour, and "instant" history.

"Mother, come down here, will you? I want you to watch this program with me," Vicki called from the basement one evening. It was a program on sex education, clear, frank, and thoroughly instructive. We had a long talk afterward.

"See what I mean, Mother? I learn all I know about life in America right here," she said. "I'm such a fish out of water with those kids at school. You have to know what their slang words mean. Most of all, you have to know what to talk to them about."

She was going through a difficult adolescence. "If our conversations were dialogue for a television show, they'd be hilarious, but this isn't funny," said Fred, after one of our head-on collisions with our daughter.

"You can say that again." The new expression had slipped out with no conscious effort on my part.

I agonized over Vicki's misery. All that meant home to her was in India. Haverstraw–Stony Point High was a foreign country—at times a hostile foreign country. It was certainly a country about which we knew nothing. We were totally unprepared to help her and what we said in the attempt was worse than no help at all.

"Accept your past," I told her. "Don't be afraid to mention your life in India. People won't think you're a queer."

"That's all you know about it," she replied. "And don't use that word 'queer' as a noun. It means something entirely different from what *you* mean by it."

I did not pursue the subject.

Sue Warner, her roommate at Woodstock School in India, visited us later. I talked to her about Vicki's difficulties.

"Mrs. Scovel, you have no idea how hard it is," said Sue. "Certain subjects, certain ways of saying things, are taboo, and you have absolutely no way of knowing which are taboo and which aren't, except by making a fool of yourself a hundred times a day. Religion is out—anything spiritual or deep —unless you get to know a person very well. Travel is completely out. You wouldn't dare say, 'When we were in Paris,' for instance."

"Why not, for heaven's sake?"

"The kids would write you off as a snob. There are places where you don't even mention New York City."

We were thankful that Vicki made friends quickly wherever she went. She made her adjustments to high school; probably none of her many friends there realized that she was not perfectly content, even happy to be where she was. But it was not easy to go to school in the morning, nor to come home to an empty house in the afternoon.

I had vowed I would never do this to any of our children. But Vicki had insisted, and Fred had agreed, that I should take the job that had been offered me. "Don't be silly, Mother," Vicki had said I'll only be here alone from three-thirty till six, and some days I may not even get home before five. I'm a big girl now. Remember?"

She *was* a big girl, but not quite as big as she thought. I took the job for four days a week. When I called her for school in the morning, she would open her eyes and ask,

"What day is it?" If I said "Wednesday," she would say, "Then you'll be here when I get home. Wednesday is the best day in the week."

In three short years, she had another adjustment to make. In September, 1962, we drove her to Tusculum College in Tennessee. After we had found her room and been on a tour of the campus, she said, "I'm all unpacked and you've seen everything, so maybe I'd better go now and see what I can do for the kids. I feel sorry for them, leaving home for the first time. I know how awful that first night can be."

I clung to the memory of Dr. Lee Vincent's words to me, long before Vicki was born. I had asked this noted educator for advice, fearing what missionary life would do to our first three children. "Every adjustment your child has to make will help to prepare him for every other adjustment in life," she had said. As I watched the back of our youngest disappear into the dormitory, I hoped she was right, oh I hoped so.

We drove back to an empty house, so quiet that Fred's long sigh filled the living room. I went into Judy's room, flung a coat across the bed, dropped gloves and hat on the bureau, handbag on the chair, to muss up the pristine neatness. Upstairs in Vicki's room, I cleaned thoroughly and made up the bed with clean sheets and bedspread to smooth away the nostalgic disorder. Downstairs again, I burst into tears as I dropped her soiled napkin in the dirty clothes hamper and put the last one of our children's napkin rings into the drawer with the others.

Fred put his arms around me. "Thanksgiving will be here in no time," he whispered in my hair. "And we are on our honeymoon."

So we were. By the time Judy phoned from Oxford, Ohio, to see how we were "adjusting," we could answer honestly that we were having the time of our lives. "We've been to the supermarket and bought lobster and mushrooms and avocados and all the things you children never wanted to eat," I told her.

"*Of course* they're expensive," said her father in answer to her question, "but we have to have *some* compensations."

"And there are only seventy-three more days before you'll be home for Thanksgiving," I added.

Little by little, we learned a small part of the anguish our older four had suffered in their adjustments to life in America. True, it had been more difficult for some than for others. It may have been easiest for Anne. "I get furious when my friends say, 'I'll never do to my children what your parents did to you,'" she said. "I tell them I wouldn't exchange my childhood in China for two of theirs in this country. They just don't realize all they've missed."

But for all of them there had been no home, no familiar ground to touch down upon for renewal, not even during the long school vacations. I wondered if, knowing what we now knew, we could ever have left them alone for those years. And we still knew very little. We could not ask questions or probe. We respected the children's silences, feeling that they would tell us what they wanted us to know.

Margaret Thompson, a fellow-missionary in Canton, once said, "You will find that this is a situation in which there is no right way. You cannot leave your children and you cannot leave your husband. You have to accept being continually torn apart emotionally, and make each decision as the circumstances arise."

In the few short years we had been in America, I had already learned that being a career woman raised the very same questions of the emotional necessity for being in two places at the same time.

❧ XIV ❧

It was on the night of March 1, 1960, when the telephone rang and the happiest man on earth anounced, "It's a girl! She's *wonderful!* So is Faith! So is everybody! So is the world!"

Further phone calls throughout the week revealed that the Rev. Carl Scovel had not come down to earth until it was time to preach the following Sunday morning, and some who heard him believed he was still airborne then. A close second were the grandparents of little Helen Scovel.

Fred and I wanted so much to experience fully the arrival of the first of our new generation. Here we were, in the United States for the great event, but we couldn't get to Sudbury, Massachusetts, to play our part in it. Instead, we flew through a blizzard to keep a speaking engagement in Chicago.

"We'll go as soon as we get back," said Fred. But another week of work and another Sunday of speaking intervened, and the following Monday Fred and my brother Bob were called to Albany. Our sister Helen was in the hospital and a consultation of doctors was necessary. The diagnosis Fred brought back was not reassuring.

"You'd better go to Sudbury alone," said Fred.

"I can't go to see our first grandchild without you."

"Honey, you know I want to go with you, but I should stay

here to be on hand if Helen's doctor phones."

"Then I should stay here, too?"

"Not at all; there's nothing imminent. I just want to get his report. But you'd better go ahead now, while you can. I'll phone you at Sudbury if there is any change and you can come directly to the hospital in Albany."

So I flew alone to the joy of holding a new little Scovel in my arms. Returning to the office next morning, I praised God for all the technology and the integrity of workmanship that had gone into the air industry, making it possible for me to have those brief hours with an armful so very precious, so very near to heaven.

And deadlines or no deadlines, I dropped everything and went to Albany that week to spend a day with my sister. She would not admit that anything was really wrong with her and insisted she'd be home in a few days. She asked for no quarter. Her emotions were kept submerged by the icy barricade she had raised to block them.

"I'll be back in a few days," I said.

"You'd better 'stick to your knitting,' " she replied. It was our father's expression for keeping us on the job. But though she said it sternly—as he would have said it—the ice melted enough to show us what we both knew.

Another speaking engagement, made months before, was scheduled for the following Sunday. "Keep the appointment," said Helen's doctor. Though I did not want to do so at all, I "stuck to my knitting." My host and hostess at Newtown Square, Pennsylvania, the Rev. and Mrs. George K. Davies, were a bulwark of strength. But when every face in the congregation looked up at me with Helen's face, I knew our sister had left us.

Birth and death, the joy of a new child to love and the sorrow of separation; it was the warp and woof of life, I knew. But the height of our joy and the depth of our sorrow closed us in a circle that somehow became a separate world of its own. And though our first grandchild had not been named for my sister Helen, I was glad she had my sister's name.

Two months later, Anne and John had a chubby little redhead, whom they named David Scovel Fitch. This time the office deadlines were such that I could take a week of my vacation to be with Anne, who needed me.

"Can't you stay another week?" she asked. No one ever came nearer to chucking a "career" than I did at that moment.

"But it must be fun to be dressed up all the time," said Anne, who looked like a fashion model in jeans, evening dress, or maternity sacks. "I like to think of you and Daddy driving off together with your briefcases every morning. Don't you just love it?"

We did "just love it." And now that the children were all away, I was especially grateful that I did not have to stay in that empty house alone. It was good to be in the front seat beside Fred, commuting to a challenging job that would keep me from feeling sorry for myself.

When people commiserated with Fred for having to drive eighty miles a day, he would say, "How many people get to go for an hour's drive with their wives every morning and evening on a road as beautiful as the Palisades Interstate Parkway?" Each season had its "spectaculars"—blossoming fruit trees and dogwoods in the spring, fields of daisies and black-eyed Susans in summer, the unbelievable glory of autumn—a sight we had been longing to see all the years we were in Asia, as were the dark evergreens against winter snow. No two mornings or evenings were alike.

Admittedly, there were days of terribly difficult driving— over ice, in deep snow, through sheets of rain or fog. And speed still terrified me when the traffic got thick. At times I was near to panic. Then I would try to remember the little

card a nun had sent me. It read, "All thy ways are pleasant-
ness and all thy paths are peace."

And the police cars! I was fascinated by them and their
occupants. "Look, there's a policeman!" I'd say.

"So what?" Fred would reply. "I'm not doing anything
wrong."

"I know you're not."

"Then why this preoccupation with policemen? You can
spot one anyplace. Sometimes I think you imagine them."

I couldn't explain it to myself or Fred. Perhaps it was because I knew the police here were *for* us. All those years of
the Sino-Japanese War and during the Communist regime in
China, the police had been against us. We were frightened
when we saw them coming. But these fine-looking clean-cut
men on our highway were there to help us—to keep the road
safe for us.

"And I think all of us commuters should cooperate with
them," I said more than once. "Yet every single car on this
road is breaking the law."

"You're allowed to go five miles over the speed limit," said
Fred.

"Who says so? I think the idea is ridiculous. Either there is
a speed law or there isn't one. No wonder there are so many
accidents."

"Accidents are caused by wives riding their husbands until
their blood pressure gets high," said Fred. "Where'll we have
lunch this noon?"

"Let's pick up some coffee and a sandwich at Chock Full
O' Nuts and eat on one of those benches near the park," I
suggested.

"Let's eat *in* the park," said Fred.

"Didn't you get that interoffice memo saying it wasn't
safe?"

Then I remembered. "Drat! I've got a date with the boss to
go over a letter we're getting out."

"Tell him you're sorry you can't make it; you've having lunch with your present husband."

"Somehow, I think it might be wiser to wait and have lunch with my present husband tomorrow; that is, if he'll be present."

"I can't promise. If you stand me up today, I may be out with a blonde tomorrow."

"I'll have to take that risk."

Once at the office, my lifelong passion for desk supplies was fully satisfied for the first time in my life. The paper clips in all sizes were shining brass, not rusty metal. And the paper! Oh, the paper! Stacks of it, and the sheets all the same size, even the scratch paper! The bond was a good thick bond; the onionskin did not tear when you drew it out of the typewriter. Envelopes fitted the folded paper perfectly. There were thumbtacks, scissors, assorted labels, pads, pencils, erasers, pens, the new felt markers in all colors, staplers (even a staple remover!). All this at my disposal without having had to count out the pennies to buy them. And as if this were not heaven enough for a writer, the coffee cart came around every morning.

In the large office I was using temporarily, the floor was carpeted. Later we learned that "status" had crept into our organization. The word was new to the overseas mission of our church, where the most inexperienced newcomer and the most knowledgeable old-timer received the same salary, housing, and perquisites.

"Four Seventy-five" (as the building was called, from its address on Riverside Drive) came as a decided shock to most of us missionaries returning from overseas. Arriving in America, we looked at once for the familiar, for the people and the places we had remembered with such affection. "One Fifty-six" (Fifth Avenue) was such a place. Instead, we came directly from our institutions, which needed funds so badly, to this magnificent building with air conditioning, wall-to-wall carpeting, new furniture, and with draperies the rumored price of which would have paid the year's salary of one of our teachers in China. The larger offices, with a view of the Hudson River, housed the higher executives and were inevitably christened the "Gold Coast."

Even the weather was regulated for us. Fresh air needed no conditioning in our estimation; but then, we had not been living where fresh air was no longer fresh. By this continued regulation of weather, most homes and all public buildings were too hot for us in winter and too cold in summer. I could never figure out what to wear. It did no good to listen to weather reports or to watch them on TV. We had no idea what a dew point was, or a frontal system or a jet stream or a T.H.I. Brother Li's weather card was easier to follow. If the little boy's pants were *blau,* it was pretty sure to be *shon* in New York City, forty miles away. I could still note whether or not the leaves were showing their silver backs, the swallows flying low, and the robins singing for rain, in which case I took an umbrella. And I could always look at the sky. Apparently no one did that anymore. If the weatherman said it would not rain, the umbrellas were left at home, though the clouds above were ready to burst and often did. "But *he said* it would be fair," was the indignant reaction heard on the elevators.

Air conditioning had an added difficulty for me. The windows were closed and could not be opened. This did not help my claustrophobia, brought on by our months in the concentration camp. Some days I would have to leave my desk and get out of the building to look at the sky for a few minutes.

But air conditioning made for efficiency. I, who could rarely write during the summer heat, easily produced as much as in winter. And though we were tempted to resent the whole idea of the move to the new building, we became more reconciled when we learned the facts. The money for the new building did *not* come from the Church's giving to the ongoing overseas mission. The building at "156" was over sixty years old and had become increasingly inadequate. To renovate, modernize, and air condition the building would have cost approximately two million dollars. By selling it and using also the funds set aside for renovation (or a new building), it was possible to take advantage of the opportunity to join with other denominations and agencies in erecting The Interchurch Center. The funds thus made available had also covered the costs of moving, the partitioning of offices, and the purchase of the new furniture. We felt better.

The building was certainly a stimulating place. Looking around the cafeteria for an empty spot at a table, we might sit beside a tenant from the World Council of Churches; see a man across the room in the dress of the Eastern Orthodox Church; talk to an employee of the American Hymn Society or to a worker in the Jewish Theological Seminary's Office for Development; be asked to write the children's service for the World Day of Prayer by an attractive member of the office of United Church Women; chat with a student working part time in Columbia University's Office of Controller, or ask a young man about the new computers in the offices of the National Aeronautics and Space Administration. A casual conversation might save duplicating a job the Methodists were doing, or present a new idea for cooperation in a project, or reveal the very statistic you'd been searching for.

And "475" was a witness. A friend of ours had lunch with a Kashmiri Muslim, who was impressed by the number of people in the building who were working for God.

"Nearly three thousand people!" he said. "In Kashmir, that many extra people would cause a famine. I ponder this. I pondered this when I was in America before. When I got back to my country, I found the solution. We are thinking only of ourselves in Kashmir. God is not such a fool. He takes care of those who love Him and give themselves to Him."

Perhaps the building should never have been called The Interchurch Center. (We had heard it called The Protestant Vatican.) It might better have been called the Time-Life Building. The offices had far more to do with life and with time (or timelessness) than with what we usually thought of as churches.

We soon got used to the building. It became simply the place where we worked. It did not even look "posh" to us any more. I got so I could leave the office on an errand without turning off all the lights. I used scratch pads instead of the backs of old letters. I even made long-distance phone calls, when time was at stake, without agonizing over the difference between the cost of the call and an airmail stamp. But something went out of my life when I was no longer aware of all that was mine. As the taxi driver said one day on the way to Kennedy Airport, "Lady, sometimes I think awareness is the greatest thing in the world. If you're unaware of something, it don't exist, it just ain't there. Like the love of your wife, her good meals, the sky, the sun. It's all there, but if you ain't aware of it, it ain't there for you, that's for sure."

✣ XV ✣

"Do you have any photos that would be good for the A.MA. exhibit?" It was Fred on the phone, "You know, something besides those six gowned figures with their hands and hardware in somebody's abdomen?"

"How about Carl Friedericks examining a patient in Nepal?" I asked.

"Carl would be the first to say, 'Not that one again.' "

"I'll ask the film library and see what they can find."

Since we had already given most of our lives to the medical mission of the Church, I was glad that our new work was along the same lines and enabled us to continue working together—Fred in the Christian Medical Council for Overseas Work, now part of the National Council of the Churches of Christ, and I in a two-year promotional program on the needs of the medical mission, for our United Presbyterian churches across the country. At the moment we were helping the American Medical Association's Department of International Health to set up a special program highlighting the work of missionary doctors, for the forthcoming annual meeting.

The phone again, and Fred. "When you find that photo will you send it up to Harold Gallina? He's going to be setting up the exhibit. I've got to go to a meeting of Interchurch Medical Assistance."

Interchurch Medical Assistance was a plan conceived by

Fred's beloved predecessor, Dr. Douglas Forman, aimed at consolidating the requests from overseas for drugs and equipment. With Arthur Wilde as able Director, drug companies and others responded with enthusiasm. In less than a year, over two million dollars worth of drugs had been given for free distribution and sent overseas through Church World Service and Lutheran World Relief.

"If Doug was looking down at that meeting, there's a mighty happy man in heaven tonight," Fred said on the way home. "I'm going to continue his conferences for doctors and nurses on furlough this year, too. Remind me to check dates with you so we can plan a July vacation as soon as it's over. Okay?"

"By that time will all the finances of the year be settled, so we can enjoy ourselves?" I asked.

"They'd better be," said Fred. Raising the funds for his program was the part of his job he thoroughly disliked, but he had the satisfaction of seeing the Christian Medical Council out of the red for the first time in some years.

One day when my phone rang, a voice with a much-put-on accent sang a Punjabi song in English—"Those days were very, *very* beautiful, ahhhhh!"

"Kundan Lall," I shouted into the phone, "Dr. Kundan Lall, where are you?"

"Right here in *Papaji's* office," he replied. "He's out just now, but his secretary is calling him."

"I'll be right down," I told him.

Dr. Kundan Lall was Professor of Ear, Nose, and Throat at the Christian Medical College in Ludhiana. He was in this country to work exclusively in the field of ear surgery with Dr. Jack Hough of Oklahoma City. Kundan Lall knew I would recognize him from the song he had sung, at popular insistence, at the Christmas parties we gave every year in India.

"I don't know how much we accomplished as missionaries," I said, after the big hug I couldn't resist giving him,
"but all of the Ludhiana people coming through here remember our Christmas parties."

"Do you know what impressed me most, above all the
other good things that *Papaji* did? He always carried that
heavy electrocardiograph machine himself, instead of getting
a coolie to do it for him."

We had a wonderful "reminisce" until Fred returned and
the two got down to business.

"Another one of your beloved Indian doctors?" asked
Pixie, my secretary, when I got back to the office. "One thing
I like about this place is that you can meet people from any
country of the world in these corridors."

"How would you like a job working nine days a week?"
asked Dr. Archie Crouch, one day in March, 1961. (The
Medical Emphasis program was to end in mid-July.) We
talked about it in his office—the Office for Communications. I
would be writing a newspaper, *Current News of the Church
Overseas;* doing articles for the magazines *Presbyterian Life*
and *Concern;* writing promotional pamphlets, and so forth.
"In other words, you'd be Special Assignments Writer,"
said Dr. Crouch.

I did not look at him once during the whole interview and
wondered later if he thought I was one of those people who
couldn't look a man in the face. An oil painting, hanging on
the wall behind him, held my visual attention as I listened to
the job description. It was "modern"—done by an Australian
woman, Lynda McNeur, I learned later.

Fred and I were fascinated by the new art in America,
never having seen anything like it in China or India. Some of
what we saw was hideous, much inconsequential; but a few of
the paintings gave us a lot of pleasure after we had learned to

stop asking, "What is it all about?" We came to the conclusion that this new expression was good *if* the artist really had something within him worth expressing. We did not have to know what that something was. If he had it, we felt it. Art was to be enjoyed, or so it seemed to me.

"You may be right," said Fred, "but not many seem to enjoy it. People appear to be critical, as if to show how much they know."

"That's true, but then, the 'chief end of man is to glorify God and enjoy Him forever,' and not many people seem to enjoy Him, either. It's too bad."

With this as background, I did not search the large canvas in Dr. Crouch's office for meaning, but before I knew it, meaning began to emerge.

People were moving from the darkness on the left toward the brightness on the right. And the brightness was—why, the Church. That could only be a church window. Inside the edifice were more people, all of them looking up, not out at those coming toward them from the darkness. Some of these had already turned away; a few still stood, undecided. There was a complete lack of communication between those inside the church and those on the street outside. Lynda McNeur may not have had this intention as she painted, but her finished work made me decide that *communicating,* and helping others to communicate, was the most important thing I could do.

"We would hope to have you come September first," said Dr. Crouch. The timing was perfect. We could attend Tom's Color Day at Wooster and watch him run his track meet (which he seemed to want us to do more than see him graduate). I could even get in six weeks of work on the children's book for Friendship Press. I must have murmured something to Archie Crouch, because I *did* go to work in the Office for Communications on September 1, 1961.

And then began friendships that endured beyond the pressures of deadlines, the discouragement of rewrites, the humiliations of boners, and the suffocation of piled-up work. At times I got so mad I could have "spat in somebody's eye," and the feelings were without doubt mutual. But it never touched our basic respect and admiration for each other and for our boss, whose small-boned body was articulated by steel nerve-wires and who drove himself harder than he drove any of us. And we learned, in times of personal difficulties or bereavement, that through those nerve-wires flowed unlimited understanding and a deep concern for what happened to us.

After six weeks in the sheltered cove of wifehood and motherhood, I was now back in the world arena, surrounded by people—all kinds of people. I kept wondering what they thought and unashamedly eavesdropped on elevators, in the washrooms, at the cafeteria. Bits of information would have made textbook models for the opening lines of stories:

"He's one of Geneva's golden-haired boys."

"That's just it; we work all the time so we can afford the things we now have no time to enjoy."

"If he'd done that to me, I'd have killed him."

Working alone at home over the years had laid the rails for a one-track mind. Now I had to get used to being interrupted by conversations, every one of which began with "I-know-I-shouldn't-interrupt-you-but." I was so interested to know what my visitors were about to tell me that it was no deprivation to put aside the papers and listen.

Mary Nack had worked in the old building at "156." We had known each other for years. "What you said at prayers this morning made me think of something," she began. "Balance. Balance is renewal. Nature is a continuing renewal—a shedding and a replacing."

"And that's what we have to do to adjust to this constantly

changing world?" I ventured. "I'm all for the shedding."

"It's the old story of preparation and acceptance. We have to prepare for life and accept it. Then the rewards come. Watch nature. Trees bend during a storm, then straighten and are as strong as ever." She made the gestures with her hand. "With time all things adjust, balance. You should write about this."

"These are your thoughts, Mary. You are the one to write them down."

With the new generation of co-workers I was often left floundering.

"Mrs. Scovel, may I speak to you a minute?" asked one of our talented young staff members, who was about to leave us for a better position.

"Another poem you've written?" I asked. "You'll have to send them to me after you leave."

"No poem this time. What do you think of premarital sexual relations?"

Some saint must have clapped a hand over my mouth. I did not gasp. I wouldn't have dared to ask such a question at her age. I wondered if then I had even known it happened. But because I liked her so much, I was pleased that she felt she could ask me the question. I told her frankly why I thought it didn't bring satisfaction or happiness, even if you could successfully rid yourself of the guilt complex, which most people couldn't. Love was caring very much what happened to the other person. And marriage was sharing responsibilities as well as joys. We talked for longer than we should have, and I never knew whether or not she felt the time had been wasted.

The frankness of the young took some getting used to, after the reticence of the Orient. Words I had had to look up in a medical dictionary when I became a nurse were now part of an everyday vocabulary.

"Beatnik" was a new word, too, and there were those who

thought it was a dirty one. Though I was a "square," my heart went out to the beatniks.

"These kids are crying for attention and nobody is answering them," I said to Fred, after a trip on a bus with a group of them.

"What do you mean?" he asked.

"Think of all the things that make a mother maddest—the ways you can be one hundred per cent sure of getting a rise out of her," I said. "Dirt. The result is sure to be, 'Go wash your hands.' 'Wipe your feet.' 'Look at that shirt.' And long hair. 'For heaven's sake get down to that barbershop.' "

"Then you think it's simple rebellion?" asked Fred.

"I think it's a cry of anguish," I replied. "They're saying, 'Look at us. For God's sake (and they mean it reverently) *look at us!*' And our only reply is, 'Disgusting.' Is it because we no longer have the answers to give them?"

"We know where to go to get the answers," said Fred.

"But how do you tell this generation about God? We've lost the ability to communicate with them."

"I wonder how far back we got off the track," said Fred. "If we could find that out, we'd know how to begin to make the contact again."

The more we heard the lyrics these young people were singing—songs to call us to repentance, quotations from Scripture to point up their meanings, impassioned pleas for peace, for freedom for all men—the more we realized that *they* had not lost the ability to communicate.

"Archie, sometimes I think Jeremiah was a beatnik," I said to my boss one morning. "These youngsters are prophets of doom. They really are prophetic in their utterances. We in the church need to hear them. Where do we begin?"

"It's hard to know," he replied. "We *must* listen to them, and we certainly have the opportunity. But they'll lose their prophetic quality if we try to fit them into our molds. We must leave them free to be the prophets."

Soon after our conversation, I had an errand in the office of a concerned young artist. On his wall hung the traditional picture of Christ—the kind I heard one boy call, "the Breck shampoo Christ." In this picture, He was walking toward us through wheat fields ready for harvest. In His hands he carried a steel guitar, so naturally that one had to look twice to see that it had been pasted on. This time my saint did not have to snap shut my sagging jaw. I was not shocked. Looking into Christ's eyes, I knew.

"Yes. Yes!" I said. "That's just where He would be today, with these ardent young people."

"That's just where He *is* today," said the artist.

One could not help wishing more of them knew it. Much that we saw evoked anything but enthusiasm. But the folk music, the overwhelming response to the Peace Corps, and the new breed of men called astronauts were like clean winds blowing across our home country.

With the coming of the civil rights movement, we were suddenly conscious of the Negroes among us.

⊶ XVI ⊷

If anyone had asked if there were Negroes working in our offices, we would have said "Yes," and would have thought immediately of Dr. Frank Wilson, Secretary for Education, with the responsibility for our involvement in the eight hundred institutions overseas to which we were related. But we would have thought of him only because he was an outstanding Negro, former Dean of Howard University, Washington, D.C., a man with a brilliant mind, beloved and respected by all of us.

The rest of the Negroes were ordinary people just like us and it would have taken a little thinking to go down the rows of offices and decide which of us were and which of us weren't Negroes. Now they stood out. We watched them. We were on their side, but did they know it? Some of us went out of our way to be "nice" to them, which must have been very painful for the Negroes. If a few friends sat down together at a table in the cafeteria, the rumors started that a plot was hatching—that "475" was one of the targets, and any day now, we whites would be wiped out. It must have been slightly amusing to our Negro friends to see white people scared, for a change. With the human rights of the Negro in America so very long overdue, I could not help feeling that we whites deserved anything we got. But then, we Scovels had been "the enemy" in a country before this, and perhaps it was easier for us, who had lived through two wars, to realize that the innocent have always had to suffer with the guilty.

Then a light broke upon us all—we had a vision of how spiritually great America could be, for a great American emerged as a leader among us and that man was a Negro. It was August of 1963 and Martin Luther King was leading a march on Washington. Our fears were not over, but we were suddenly bound together in a cause that made it seem worth while to die or, what can be harder yet, to be hurt and maligned by those who did not understand our motives.

"Four-seventy-five" became a frenzy of activity. Literally thousands of sandwiches were made, busses were hired, plans set for doubling up on the office work so that all who wished to go would be free to do so. I waited to see what Fred would say. I was just back at work after being in bed with a bad back, and I feared he would count me out, no matter how much I pleaded.

"Are you going?" I asked.

"Of course," he replied.

"Why?"

"Because I feel I ought to be there, that's all."

"Can't I go with you? I'll be careful."

"With all that crowd, even a little push might throw your back off again," he said, "and nobody really knows what's going to happen."

Nobody knew what was going to happen. It was my reason for wanting desperately to go. If Fred was going to be in danger, I wanted to be near him, as I had been through all the perilous experiences of our past.

Carl phoned from Sudbury. He told us a little about his work for human rights, then said, "I thought you'd like to know I'm going to Washington."

My besetting sin, imagination, jumped into the breach. How would Faith manage if anything happened to Carl?

Baby Christopher was only a year and a month old and Helen a little over three. I was proud of Carl, of course, but I wanted to build that selfish little wall of safety around my two men.

Judy, Vicki, and I got up very early to see Fred off. We couldn't let him go, and ran from the back door to the front to wave again as he came around the driveway. Just opposite the front door, he stopped the car for what we supposed would be a last good-by. He lowered the car window, leaned out, and called, "Don't forget to put out the garbage."

"We might have known," said Judy.

We watched that blessed invention, television, all day; and as we watched, we realized that something was happening—the miracle of brotherhood was being enacted before our eyes. Among all that throng of people, not an incident occurred, except when one man tried to speak without permission. He was quickly and quietly taken away.

"There were about two-hundred-ten thousand of us," Fred said when he got home, "a third of them white. And everyone of us was deeply moved. I really didn't expect anything more than a long walk in the hot sun—well, I don't know how to describe it except to say that it was a spiritual experience."

In the office next day the previous tense excitement had disappeared. A quiet wonder had taken its place. All anyone could talk about was what had happened the day before—to those of us watching, as well as to those marching.

"I don't know what it was, but it did something to you inside," said one of the young secretaries, as she redid her lashes in the Ladies Room.

"It felt as if the Holy Spirit were hovering over us," said a furloughed missionary.

"I stood next to a rabbi who kept shouting, 'Hallelujah,' " said an executive from the "Gold Coast."

There was a hush of hallelujahs upon all we did that day. There was no "Gold Coast," no carpeted or uncarpeted offices. We were drawn together by a common experience. For that one day, we were really communicating with one another.

Archie had not been joking when he spoke of a job nine days a week. Every year I would say to myself, "Next year will be easier." And every year there was more to do than there had ever been before. Many mornings I was up at five to write before going to work. I wrote continuously through vacations, holidays, and some weekends. Most of this was my own fault. Everything I did gave me an idea for something else.

Only a man as patient and understanding as Fred could have endured such a wife. He insisted on having someone come in once a week to do the cleaning. I washed, ironed, and cooked at night, and enjoyed the tasks that did not call upon any powers of creativity. By the next morning I would be ready, when Archie came in with an idea for a new article, to say, "Yes, I can work it in," only to find that it was one more sheet of paper in the ever increasing stack of things yet to be done. I was a long time in accepting the fact that much of that stack would never be touched—a far cry from my life as a nurse, when everything had to be done before going off duty.

"I feel like the man in the parable who said he'd go into the vineyard and never went," I told Archie.

"It's better to have more ideas than you can complete than the other way around," he said.

Sometimes I doubted it. There were days when I almost dared to pray, "Please, God, not one more idea." I wanted so much to lead a simple, uncluttered life, to "zero in" on "one thing at a time and that done well."

Fred was tired, too. "And I have to go to work in New York when I could stay here and talk to a chickadee in the snow," he sighed one morning when he came in from feeding the birds.

Our real frustration came because we could see no end to the race which caught us up and made us run with it. Throughout the city, men were jockeying for position, trying to keep out front. The knowledge explosion was jet propulsion behind us. Rats were being fed to increase their brain capacity; we would be next. The better our brains, the more knowledge there would be let loose and the greater the speed required to keep up with it—a speed which gave us no time to make choices.

The cry was for change, any change. Men's positions depended upon whether or not they came up with a continual stream of new ideas. No longer did anyone meditate, people simply reacted. If thinking was to be done, one man of the group was chosen to be the "think person." Long-range planning was the daily task, and the plans were obsolete before they were fully formulated. Men vied with one another to be "farthest out" in their thinking, yet what seemed to me to be no more than the obvious next step in long-range planning by a Church concerned with mission, was considered *too* far out.

"What were we as Christians planning to do about the invasion of our planet from outer space?" was the question I wanted answered. The thought came to me with new intensity upon reading a note I found on my kitchen table one evening when we got home from work. Dear Hazel Peifley cleaned our house once a week out of the goodness of her heart (and somewhat against the wishes of Harold, her husband). I rarely saw her, as she came on Thursdays when I was in New York, but we wrote notes to each other, and I always enjoyed reading Hazel's.

"Dear Mrs. Scovel," she wrote on one occasion. "I was one of those many people to see that funny object in the sky on Monday night. After all the times of hearing others talk about these things and never before having seen anything like it, something made me look toward the window just as it was going by. I called to the rest of the family, but it went so fast no one else could see it.

"And it gave me a good feeling, for as I went to bed, I thought, 'Will it happen to me like that when Jesus comes? How wonderful it will be for His Chosen Ones to see!'"

Here, at last, was one woman who was not afraid of "the little green men from Mars." (They were probably not from Mars. "And they are *not* 'little green men,'" said Alice Roosevelt, who knew more about the voyagers from outer space than anyone I knew. "Some of them are ten feet tall.")

Perhaps "flying saucers" could be explained away, but here we were, spending billions of dollars exploring outer space; able to overcome all the technological problems involved, finding men courageous and adventurous enough to undertake the journey, and yet we were unimaginative enough to refuse to consider that we might find an inhabited planet, or that "they" knew as much as we did and had already found us.

I had read of landings upon our earth and of personal encounters which seemed credible. From the reports, some of these "humanoids" had been kind. Was it too difficult to believe that our God was the God of the Universe and more? If he was God, he *had* to be. I wanted someone to go over the literature and see if there was any clue to the spiritual reactions of these "people." More than this, I wanted some thought given to how we, as Christians, should greet the visitors. Was the Church preparing for its mission in outer space? Was the Church preparing to *receive* a mission from outer space? Or would those who came to our planet find only fear.

We had seen fear breed hideous consequences in our world.

But the Church was caught up in the mad race too. Who had time to think out a mission for space? "Can't you hear me being hooted out as a real crackpot?" asked one of my colleagues. "Boy, would I ever lose my job." Fear, again.

"Maybe we made our first mistake when the Church tried to keep up with Madison Avenue," said Fred, as we drove home that night.

"I wonder what would happen if we had never settled in New York City," I said. "If the whole United Presbyterian Commission on Ecumenical Mission and Relations had moved to a place where we didn't even know what other denominations, or even our own agencies were doing. Would we develop creative ideas without worrying about having to come up with something better than the fellows in the office next door?"

"Some place like Big Moose Lake?" asked Fred.

"Some place like Big Moose Lake," I replied. "But then, it wouldn't belong to us any more."

"Let's be selfish and not suggest it," said Fred.

❧ XVII ❧

"Shall we let them in on it?" asked Bea Goode, N.C.C. Far Eastern Office.

"I don't know; it takes a special kind of person," replied Abby Jacobs, U.P. Mass Communications Overseas.

Fred and I were sitting at a table in the cafeteria with these two young, graying petites. We had been talking about vacations. Where would we go?

"It's got to be some place where we can be alone; where we can hike and swim and read," said Fred, "and where we won't have to socialize."

"I've got a book to finish," I added.

"And she has to be where she won't be interrupted by someone wanting her to do something else all the time," said Fred.

"Well then, it's okay," said Abby. "Not everyone would be happy at the place we go. We love it, but there's nothing 'going on' there, if you know what I mean."

"Sounds perfect," I said.

"Write to Mr. Howard Martin, The Waldheim, Big Moose, New York," said Bea. "Tell them we suggested it."

In due time, a cordial letter from Mrs. Martin arrived. We packed corduroys, sweaters, and walking shoes; a box of books, Fred's recorder and pastels; my typewriter, manuscript, and stacks of paper. During the last week at the office, we held our breath every time the phone rang, for fear some emergency would arise that would keep us from getting away, but the day came. Judy, home from college, and Vicki both got up early to kiss us good-by; last-minute housekeeping instructions were flung back from the car window and we were off.

Up the Thruway to Utica, north and east on routes 12 and 28 to Old Forge and Eagle Bay, then northwest on a narrow, bumpy road. "Keep to the right whenever there's a fork," Bea's instructions read. "You'll come to a T. Turn right and go straight ahead till you hit the dirt road. Go to the end of the dirt road and pull the road in after you. You're there."

"Look, there's the lake. I didn't know it would be so big," I said, as we drove down a steep incline into a forest of giant evergreens and smaller maples, beeches and golden birches. Wild flowers and ferns carpeted the hollows. Delicate new leaves of the higher bushes floated in a golden haze.

"The smell!" Fred exclaimed. "I haven't inhaled that smell of the Adirondacks since Charlie Davis and I worked at the lumber camp that summer."

Wanda Martin, tall, lithe, with blonde curls at her neck, came out to meet us from the first of a row of bark-covered log houses edging the lake. They looked like small Swiss chalets. We drove part way through the woods, then walked to "Long View," our own particular chalet on North Bay.

Inside the living room with its comfortable chairs and sofa, a fire was crackling in the huge fireplace, its glow washing highlights across the sheen of the log rafters above. Howard Martin came in with an armful of wood. He had the ultra-broad shoulders and sturdy build of a woodsman, and the twinkle in his blue eyes promised a lot of fun when we got to know him. We had found that the voices of mountain people the world over have a mellow quality rarely heard on the plains. The Martins and their three teen-agers, Jon, Nancy and Philip, whom we met later, were no exceptions.

"You'll have hot water for a bath," said Wanda Martin. "It's heated from the fireplace."

Hot water? A bath? In a tub? The chalet was complete with plumbing—my idea of the perfect way to "rough it" in the woods. She took us to the upstairs porch to show us the view. "A doe and two fawns have been coming to that little bay just below those tall evergreens on the left," she said. "Supper will be ready at six. The dining room is the first building you saw when you came in."

Fred and I stood at the railing looking out over the bay. Silence lay like peace upon the water and upon the blue-green hills beyond. "It's so quiet you can hear it," I whispered to Fred. Then we both smiled, remembering Judy's remark on such an occasion in the Himalayas, "It's so quiet I don't want to chew my carrots." That afternoon, as I sat in the long chair on the upstairs porch, I tried to read and couldn't. I had to stop every few minutes to listen to the silence.

At quarter of six, we started out through the woods on a path spongy with pine needles. Here, our feet were not rejected at every step as they were on the concrete pavements of New York. The ground accepted us, springing with us as we walked. We didn't say a word, wanting to hear every lap of the lake on the pebbled shore, every sigh of the wind through the pines. This was how God must have meant the world to be.

On the little entrance porch to the dining room stood a large stone jar filled with the white blossoms of witch hobble. We entered and were introduced to the guests. They all looked like "our kind of people," as Fred's mother used to say. But my usually sociable, gregarious husband was reduced to the inertia of cold, solid rock. When one of Howard Martin's meals (the cook had not yet arrived) warmed him only a little, I asked, "What's the matter with you?"

"I'm afraid someone will want to drop in and talk this

evening," he whispered. We needn't have worried. The guests were no more anxious to be with us than we with them. Furthermore, there was an unwritten law at The Waldheim that you did *not* drop in at another guest's cottage. Someone might say, "I'm climbing Bald Mountain tomorrow. Anyone want to join me?" He would not be at all hurt if there were no "takers."

Not a soul dropped by and no phone rang.

"Let's start our new book," said Fred. We usually kept one book going which we read aloud.

"You read, so I can knit," I urged.

"You read better than I do."

"You aren't fooling anybody by that remark, gallant sir." I picked up Robert Henri's, *The Art Spirit*.

"You read till I finish my pipe; then I will," said Fred.

Later, we made our separate choices from the box of books we had brought and read until almost twelve, reveling in the knowledge that we would not have to get up early next morning.

We settled into something of a routine. After breakfast of blueberry pancakes and sausage, I worked on my manuscript, while Fred took the difficult hikes or did a pastel. Afternoons were spent in swimming, canoeing, climbing Stillwater Mountain or the more distant Blue Mountain, or in hiking to the various lakes—Twitchell, Silver, Cascade, the Gulls. We chatted with the guests in the dining room after dinner, then sat on the dock or on the upstairs porch to watch evening wing in and settle down on the lake.

From June, 1963, on, Spring and Fall found us at The Waldheim for a week of renewal. Once Howard loaned us a Parson's Adirondack-guide boat and Fred rowed me up the lake to watch a pair of Canadian geese. Once I stopped just outside Long View to face a deer, not fifty feet from me. The deer and I stood still for what seemed like a long time, until Fred slammed a screen door at the house. All my life, I would hold to my heart that a deer had looked at me and had not been afraid.

I was never afraid in the woods until Fred got lost. Then we realized how near we were to the wilderness and how far from civilization. He had climbed to the top of Billy's Bald Spot and had lost the trail to Squash Pond. It was hours before he got himself out of the swamps and over the hills to a road, miles from camp. While I sat on the porch, helpless, Howard and Jon searched, firing off a gun or calling to give Fred word that they were looking for him. Howard came back once to see if he had returned. "The last fellow that did this was gone for three days," said Howard. "We had to call in airplanes to find him. I hope he gets back before dark." It was dusk when Fred appeared, tired and shaken.

The next morning when I awoke, there was a note on my bureau. "I'm taking the canoe to Punky Bay. Back in time for breakfast."

"Deliver me from a husband who is always seeking adventure," I groaned to myself.

"You should be glad I didn't take you and a tennis racket with me," said Fred. "That's the scene of the murder in Theodore Dreiser's *An American Tragedy.*" The murderer had been a cousin of the Gilettes of Cortland, New York, where Fred grew up.

One Spring, when the snow was still in the hollows and tiny May flowers made galaxies of the greening banks, Howard proposed a picnic. "Just the four of us," he said. "You two have never had a lumberman's breakfast." We took the motorboat up the lake and part way through the inlet. A short hike over the mountain brought us to Russian Lake, where we found an old lean-to and a campfire site.

Howard pulled a small pail of potatoes out of his pack. "You two women get to work on these," he said, handing each of us a paring knife.

"We'll never eat all these; I wouldn't have to peel this many potatoes for my whole family. Besides, I never eat potatoes," I whispered to Wanda.

"When Howard says, 'Peel potatoes,' you peel potatoes," she whispered back.

Howard was frying a pound of bacon for the four of us. We ate all the bacon and some sixteen good-sized potatoes, sliced thin and fried in the bacon fat. We drank innumerable cups of coffee, replenished from the large pot on the fire. Sitting still, watching a woodpecker, we did not notice that Howard had gone back to the fire until a few minutes later.

"What is he doing?" I asked Wanda.

"Cooking the steaks, I suppose," she answered.

"The steaks? I don't believe it," I said.

"Sure," said Howard. "This is a lumberman's breakfast, not one of those little picky orange-juice-and-cigarette jobs you people in New York call breakfast." We ate our plate-sized steaks, tender and perfectly broiled.

"I never thought I could do it," said Fred.

"Have another cup of coffee and you'll be ready for the pancakes," said Howard. "Do you folks like real maple syrup?"

We "city slickers" were not to be outdone. We polished off the pancakes like veterans. We leaned back against our separate tree trunks, and at our request, Howard told us the history of The Waldheim.

E. J. Martin, Howard's father, had come to this part of the country in 1894, when he was twenty-two years old. "He went to work on the railroad at Raquette Lake, and . . ."

We liked to listen to Howard. He conversed with the culture he had imbibed from his schoolteacher mother and did not lose at Duke University. But he could drop into the patois of a wandering Canadian Frenchman or the brogue of a visitor from Scotland. It was also rumored that he could pour out acrid brimstone when the rare occasion arose to provoke it. On this drowsy afternoon, he went on with the family history.

"Mother and Dad were married on January 22, 1902. Harriet E. Brown was my mother's name. She taught school in Port Leyden, worked up here summers. They met over at Jim Higby's where they were both working at the time. They came up here to their new home right after the wedding, in the dead of winter. Dad started to build in December. It's cold up here in December. But with the help of Uncle Charlie, Philo Smith, and Sam Vanetter, he had the house ready for his bride when they moved in the last of January."

The Waldheim took in its first guests on June 12, 1904. The old register, which Wanda and I looked through later, carried the names for that day written in a script that would do the writer proud in the years to come:

Mrs. G. W. Davis, Washington, D.C.
Mr. P. G. Mumford   "   "
Mrs. P. G. Mumford   "   "
Miss E. L. Davis   "   "
Miss Z. A. Davis   "   "
Miss Osai Tanaka   "   "

The last name intrigued us. Who was Miss Osai Tanaka of Washington, D.C.? Evidently a Japanese. There was no doubt about the Davis family. The register some weeks later carried the name, "Maj. Gen. G. W. Davis," and after it, "Gov. Gen. Panama."

A random finger down the guest column of the same register traced addresses of guests from Carnarvon, North Wales; Eureka, California; Dubuque, Iowa; Charlotte, North Carolina; Denver, Colorado; Tampa, Florida; Catherine, Ontario, Canada; Sidney, Australia.

Gradually we met the whole household. Jon and Nancy introduced us to Ivan and Boris, the two orange cats; Mike, the rabbit hound; and Lemon Seed, Nancy's horse, otherwise known as Fink. Philip showed us his ducks. Cathy, Mary Ellen, and the other girls working their way through college, waited on table and kept the cabins tidy. A phantom came in each morning to light the fire before we were up. Ed, perhaps? Or Duane, who had come up for a summer and stayed two years?

Those we came to know best were Vernon, rugged as a tree root; Anna, his dear little ball of a wife; and Leila, tall, graying, but still "blonde-complected." Vernon took care of the grounds; Anna made pies, cakes, and doughnuts that would "melt in your mouth"; Leila kept the linen as white as the arum lilies growing below the porch of her laundry. We would often sit around the kitchen table, listening to their recollections of earlier days at The Waldheim.

"We used to drive in every year with a load of maple syrup for the Martins," said Vernon. "Every year they'd buy twenty-five, thirty gallons. After we sold the farm, we came in with another load. Asked if they hired help."

"We decided we'd like to do something together," said Anna. "We talked with the Martins and they said they needed a pastry cook. I said I'd try, but I'd only done home baking."

"We used to kill the pigs in the winter and Mrs. Martin would render enough lard for shortening to last all summer. Had to feed about a hundred and forty guests, too. She was a grand woman, was Mrs. Martin," said Vernon. "More like a mother to everyone than anybody I ever knew." He stopped to refill his pipe. Anna took up the story. "She and I used to get up at half past three every morning to do the heft of the baking before the work of the day began. People ate more in those days."

"I used to make ice cream every Sunday," Vernon put in, "two quarts of heavy cream in an eight-gallon freezer. Girls all loved you. Wanted to lick the paddle."

"We worked all day," said Anna. "Maybe we'd have an hour off, say three o'clock to four in the afternoon, then we'd work straight through until everything was cleaned up and the dishes done at night. It'd be eight-thirty or so. In wintertime Mrs. Martin made rag rugs. I'd braid the strips for her."

"She could do them better than anyone I ever knew," said Leila, looking up from her knitting. "They'd lay down just as flat and perfect. We're still using them. You'll find them in some of the cottages." Leila had taken care of Mrs. Martin during her last illness.

"Do you remember a popular singer by the name of Julia Sanderson?" asked Anna. "Probably not. You were out of the country a lot. She and a fellow sang over the radio."

"They called them 'America's Sweethearts' or something like that," said Vernon. "She was a guest up here," Anna went on. "I've heard Mrs. Martin tell how Julia Sanderson would take a walk down the dirt road through the woods, wearing white shoes and a long white dress and petticoats, and come back without a speck of dirt on her. Neatest person you ever saw, Mrs. Martin used to say. In those days Mrs. Martin used to wash and starch and iron all those petticoats for the guests."

"What did E. J. do?" asked Fred.

"E. J. ran the sawmill, did the office work, made all the furniture—dressers, beds, chairs, tables—made kneehole desks for each of his grandchildren, too," said Vernon. "He designed and built all thirty-five of the buildings here, the sixteen cottages, icehouse, woodhouses and the like."

Even the sheds for wagons were beautifully built. Fred took a picture of the patterned bark-covered wood at the end of a barn. Twisted branches, carefully chosen, made the balustrades for porches; matching stones were the masonry for small bridges.

"Did you ever hear of a whipsaw?" asked Vernon.

It was also called a pit saw "because of the man in the pit below," Vernon explained. "They'd build a huge sawhorse with a slot down the middle of it, pin the log to the top, draw a chalk line down the center of the log and cut it in two lengthwise. They'd put the smooth side inside for the walls of the room and chink the cracks with moss. House up next to Long View was built that way. Built in 1900 and the moss is still in the cracks."

We finally met E. J. Martin and counted it a privilege. He was living in Schenectady with his older son, Everett, who had brought him up to The Waldheim for the weekend. While Everett got some of the boats ready for the season, E. J. followed Vernon around as he worked, or sat in the sun watching him repair a tool. We passed them several times that day, and noticed that although Mr. Martin was over ninety (as we had been told), his cheeks were firm and red, his blue eyes clear enough to let the "devilment" shine through. We were introduced that evening after dinner. Fred asked a question and got a typical E. J. Martin answer.

"Did you have a good winter?" asked Fred.

"Yes," said E. J. "Just sat around and let them look at me. Made quite a winter of it."

A resident of Old Forge once told us, "Most of the Adirondack places you go to these days you can set down in Cape Cod or Atlantic City or Miami, Florida, and never know the difference. Martin's place is the last of its kind. I hope we never lose it."

Was time running out on places like The Waldheim? We hoped with all our hearts that this was not true. But we were going back to a world in which Martin's place was as irrelevant as the dinosaur to today's scramble to the top of the heap. Or was it? No one could turn back time. No Christian would want to; God being "the first to enlighten men's minds," "the spirit that first led them out of their brutish state and made them men," as John Baillie had said. Human progress must have been part of God's plan. Left to chance, its first beginnings would never have come off. And God, being the God of history, was as creatively alive in the seething of today as in the seething genesis of the universe. Perhaps it was not too late for men to open their eyes and see the "wondrous things" that God had prepared for them.

"But God, do not let us run ahead of You, nor lag behind You," I prayed, thinking of the stinking subways. Surely God had never intended them as part of progress. Now man had found a way, not only to fly, but to skim over the ground without touching its surface. Could we have saved our spongy paths? Could we have avoided our air-polluting cars and our dirty subways if we had been listening to God for guidance in our inventing? Surely He had more possibilities for "something new and different" than had Madison Avenue. Was it possible that we could still save and *use* our rivers, our trees, our Waldheims?

"Congratulate me! I'm a grandfather!" shouted Howard, interrupting my packing as he banged delightedly on our screen door.

"Congratulations!" we both shouted back, before realizing that the possibilities of Howard's being a grandfather at that moment were exceedingly remote.

He reached into the pocket of his black-and-white-checked shirt and pulled out a wide-eyed duckling. It settled into his calloused hand as comfortably as if it were on a nest of hay. "Six of them," said Howard. "Philip's ducks have produced."

Anyone could produce at The Waldheim. The second book of the Scovel family saga was almost finished. It would be hard to say who was more relieved, Fred or I.

❧ XVIII ❧

I hated to take our vacation mornings for writing. I wanted to be free to do what Fred wanted to do. "But it's like getting hold of a charged wire," I told him. "You can't drop it until the last spark of an idea has been drained from you, no matter how hard you try."

"Of course you can't," he said. "Anyway, we have our afternoons and evenings and that's a lot to be thankful for."

"And you do have me out of your hair for a *few* hours each day."

"You mean you have me out of *your* hair. I wish you didn't have to work so hard, though. You don't get enough rest and you never have a vacation away from a desk."

It was his quiet undergirding and his persistent encouragement over the years that gave me the stamina to keep on writing. However prejudiced his judgment, he believed that I had something worth saying and the ability to say it, and he kept the challenge before me.

"Have you decided what you are going to call this book?" he asked as we were driving back to Stony Point from Big Moose Lake. "I surely am anxious to read it."

"I'd like to call it *Richer by India.* You've no idea what a relief it is to know that I haven't 'lost' India, as I feared when we first came home. The whole experience is richer since I've written it down."

"I told you India couldn't just drop out of your life."

Descending deep into memory, I saw things I had not consciously seen, and remembered more than I had consciously remembered. I even knew our friends better since I had taken time to think about what they were really like. I had enjoyed the writing, perhaps because I now knew a little more about the craft, having learned a lot from Archie Crouch and having written for many hours every day.

Far different had been the writing of *The Chinese Ginger Jars*. Prose was then completely out of my line. Fred had started me writing poetry when Jim, Carl, and Anne were aged six, four, and two.

"You've got to have a hobby or you'll go out of your mind," he'd said. Fred believed that all missionaries should have hobbies. "What's yours going to be? Stamps? Coins? Old charms?"

"Nothing that costs money," I told him. "One collector in the family is enough. Anyway, I'm a thrower-out at heart. How about poetry? I've always wanted to write poetry."

The hobby was tied to a permanent hitching post later, when Fred succeeded in accomplishing two of his purposes at once. He had been trying in vain both to encourage the writing and to get me to rest after a bout of pneumonia. I was teaching the children every weekday. (There were no suitable elementary schools in our interior Chinese city.) I did not see how I could manage either the poetry or the rest.

"I'll bring you your breakfast in bed every Saturday morning if you will have a poem on my desk by noon," he promised.

"You know very well I'll do anything for breakfast in bed."

Prose was a horse of a different color. I wanted, for the children's sake, to write down fully all that had happened to us in China during the Sino-Japanese War and under the

Communist regime. The miracles had been many. The children knew little of the background of what had occurred or of the dangers under which we had been living. We had spared them as much as we could. Now we both felt they should know the story of those years of their childhood. But I was so sure I could not write prose that I never fully faced the task until I met a young minister in the Rochester, New York, area named Luther Cross.

Luther had asked me to speak in his church on several occasions. He must have heard the whole story many times. At any rate, he begged me to write it down.

"I'll buy you a dictaphone; I'll get you a stenographer; I'll do anything to keep this story from being lost," he urged. When he learned that we were going to India, he said, dejectedly, "You'll go out there and get yourself killed, and nobody will ever hear of these miracles."

I, too, was sure that no one would ever hear the story of our life in China. How could I ever get the feeling of China, in India? Having by now given some thought to the book, it was an act of "noble renunciation" to put the writing out of my mind.

A little over a year after our arrival in India, I was climbing a steep mountain path in the foothills of the Himalayas, on my way to the summer session of language school. The whole book suddenly hit me like a landslide. The day before, we had found two Chinese ginger jars in an old junk shop in the bazaar. They had evidently started the rocks slipping, for each picture on the jars formed itself into a chapter.

Writing was agony. Each sentence had to be hewn from solid rock. I rewrote the book every year for at least four years. There was something wrong with it and I could not find out what. Not long after we were settled in our jobs in New York, I took the manuscript to Mr. Eugene Exman, editor-manager of the Religious Books Department of

Harper & Brothers, soon to be Harper & Row. I had no idea of his publishing it, since he had refused it some years before. But I needed advice as to where I should go for help.

"Have you rewritten it?" he asked.

"Several times," I replied.

"Then let us read it again. It will help us know how to advise you."

"We like it," said Mr. Melvin Arnold, later; "but we feel you should have some help in rewriting it. We've arranged to have Nelle Keys Bell work on it with you. She is one of the editors for *The Ladies Home Journal*."

The last thing I wanted was to have a "profane" hand laid upon my precious book, and I made this perfectly clear to Mr. Arnold.

"Suppose you see her first," he suggested.

It was only fair to write Nelle Keys Bell. "I'm sure you have had enough experience with authors to know that I take a very dim view of having anyone tamper with my manuscript," I wrote. "But I would like so much to talk to you. Could you possibly come to New York, or shall I meet you in Philadelphia?"

She came to New York. The moment she walked into the office, I felt as if I had known her always. She was a perky little Southerner with the zip of a New Yorker. "Mrs. Scovel, why does Harper want me to rewrite your book?" she asked. What was meant to be a Southern drawl came out a brisk staccato.

"It must be because they think you can do a better job than I," I replied.

"But you write much better than I do," she said.

Well! The last wall was down between us. She thought I could write! Nelle Keys Bell could not know what she did for me with that sentence. And she had more to give.

"I want to ask you a question. What are you afraid of?"

That was it! That was what was wrong with the book. Her question, like a sensitive forefinger, had touched the very spot. I was afraid of so many things—that our Chinese friends might be traced and punished for their association with "imperialist Americans"; that our teen-age children might be embarrassed by what I wrote of them; that the love which Fred and I felt for each other would be exposed to the world. I had tried so hard to dissemble—never describing a Chinese; calling the children by their Chinese names; designating Fred and me by simply using personal pronouns, and of course, writing the whole book in the third person.

Lost in thought, I was brought back by another question. "I want to ask, is your husband dead?" said Nelle Keys Bell. "I don't see him and I don't see any of the children. I feel your love for the Chinese people, but I don't see them as individuals. You're going to have to pull out all the stops and tell the whole story, or put the manuscript away in a bottom drawer and forget it."

"Let me think about it," I said. "It is quite a decision to make. I'm not sure I can bring myself to living in a goldfish bowl."

"It's a question only you can decide." She rose to her feet. "You know, if you and I were Hindus, we would swear we had known each other in another incarnation."

"We can almost believe it even if we aren't Hindus," I told her. "You'll be hearing from me."

"Oh, you don't need me," she insisted.

It was hard to know what to do. Daily, I asked God to let me know whether or not I should rewrite the book. Gradually ideas began to come. I could describe our Chinese friends and change their places of residence so that no one could be traced. I asked the children how they felt. Anne thought it would be fun to be in a book; Jim and Carl took the whole idea very lightly. "Now, Mother, you needn't worry," said Jim. "We're not going to be Christopher Robins."

"No, Mom," said Carl. "I don't think you need to have a care in the world that you will become that famous."

Fred and I talked about it often. "I don't want to push you into anything you don't want to do," he said one evening, "but I don't think you will ever be satisfied until you have written that book to the best of your ability."

He was right. I could not escape. One morning he said, "When are you going to write Nelle Keys Bell? You've already put six years of your life into that book, and 'No one who puts his hand to the plow and turns back is fit for the kingdom of God.' "

That very day I wrote Nelle, asking her to stay by me through the writing, which I would send her chapter by chapter. I knew that I would pull back into my shell. And I did just that. But whenever I tried to hide behind a nebulous situation, Nelle would take a sheet of yellow paper and describe what she thought had happened. I would say, *"No, it was not like that at all. It was like this!"* She could pull all of it out of me, and she also had an uncanny way of getting inside me. She often wrote the scene so well, she could only have been present in one of her "incarnations."

After all our work, we met with disappointment. Mr. Exman had asked us to send a copy of the manuscript to *The Ladies Home Journal* to see if they would publish it. Our understanding was that Harper publication depended upon its acceptance. Nelle wrote the sad news that the magazine had rejected the manuscript.

"I've lost all confidence in my editing," she said. "I was so very sure that it was a good book."

If she, with all her ability, had lost confidence, what about me? Where did I ever get the idea I could write in the first place? Fred was crushed. "After all those years of work," he said. "After all the getting up early and working late!"

Poor, poor darling. He was so despondent that I felt I *had* to find a publisher. But I no longer believed in myself enough to try. Work went on at the office, but I knew I was not doing a good job.

"You and I are going to a show," said Fred one day. "We haven't seen one since we came to New York. I think we both need something else to think about." He was able to get seats for *The Miracle Worker*, with Anne Bancroft, but neither of us was enthusiastic about going. At least a new permanent would keep me from *looking* so depressed. I took a long noon hour from the office.

Returning, I found Pixie on pins and needles. "I thought you'd never get back," she said. "Harper's has been trying to get you."

"So what?" I said. "They've probably heard that *The Ladies Home Journal* has refused the manuscript." She stood waiting while I phoned—a thing she had never done before. She could not make herself go back to her desk.

It was Mr. Arnold. "Mrs. Scovel, we are ready to start on your book," he said.

"What do you mean by that?" I asked.

"We're ready to publish it."

Then it did not matter about *The Ladies Home Journal!*

"Frank Elliott will be working with you on it. We hope to have it out in the spring of sixty-two."

Nineteen sixty-two was the year the Churches were to study China. *The Chinese Ginger Jars* would appear on the denominational book lists. I had begun the writing in 1954. Much as I had grumbled at all the intervening years of effort, I knew that, once again in my life, this was God's perfect timing.

"Do you serve tranquilizers with announcements like this?" I asked. Mel Arnold chuckled as he said good-by.

I grabbed my quiet little Pixie around the waist and danced with her to the door. I tore to the elevators, down to Fred's office, startling him from his papers, and told him the news. He jumped up, took me in his arms, and kissed me. We phoned Nelle and she was ecstatic. We phoned the children. "That's great, Mom. That's simply great," said each of the boys separately. Anne squealed with delight; Judy wanted to cry she was so happy; Vicki went out and bought me a teacup to start my collection.

Somehow, Fred and I got through the rest of that December afternoon. We went out into the coldest evening of the year and took a subway miraculously filled with sunshine. We ate at Schrafft's and walked several blocks to the theater without once having our feet touch ground. The play was the play of all plays. It was as if we had never seen one before. When the final curtain came down, we were so happy that people stared at us. We drove home through a crystal world and couldn't sleep we were so excited.

When I awoke next morning, my first thought was, "I'm an author." Fred gave me breakfast in bed to celebrate.

⚜ XIX ⚜

It was Christmas, 1964. Fred and I were getting out the tree ornaments and setting up the crèche. The car arriving was Judy's "Sweetums Red Rambler," back from the supermarket where she and Vicki had been shopping. Fred went to the door to help with the packages, but even so simple a procedure was never routine in our household.

"Look out! You've dropped the meat," he shouted, running to the rescue as the girls got out of the car, their arms full of groceries. The sight of the nude leg of lamb bounding down the little hill, wrapper flying behind it, made them laugh so hard that all their bundles were slipping.

"There goes the celery," I called. "Please! The eggs!" Between juggling and ballet, Vicki retrieved both.

"You have enough food here for an army," said Fred, back in the kitchen.

"Exactly," said Judy.

"I wonder what it would be like to have *normal* children," said their father.

"You'd be bored," said Vicki.

"Have you forgotten that this Christmas only we four will be here?" I asked. "And we're going to Bear Mountain for dinner?"

"Vicki has to have something to eat after the late show," said Judy.

"Vicki has to?" said the accused. "You mean *Judy* has to."

We were all very gay—hilarious, in fact—because this was probably the hardest Christmas we had ever had to face. It was not only because we four would be alone. Tom and Janene were teaching in Bangkok Christian College, Thailand—the first of this generation of Scovels to find their particular mission in the overseas church.

And their wedding on June 10, 1962, was the first Scovel wedding Fred and I had been in this country to attend. The two had found each other at Ohio State University, while Tom was completing his master's degree in linguistics. The family safari to see the beautiful musician, Janene Nicodemus, become the wife of our youngest son was an experience for the family album. To mention only one episode—a carload of Scovel and Nicodemus guests and bridesmaids, carrying on their laps trays of open-faced sandwiches for the reception, had taken a railroad crossing at high speed. Little did the guests realize that their canapes had been reassembled from car ceiling, doors, windows, bridesmaids' frocks, and even one guest's forehead!

We could weather the Tom Scovels' absence, knowing how happy they were—knowing too, how wonderful a mission Christmas could be. We would weather the absence of the rest of the young marrieds, for we had known all along that this was their year to spend Christmas with the other in-laws. What we could not weather was the black storm of depression whose full strength had fallen upon our husband and father.

Three days before Christmas, Fred had learned the facts of what he had been fearing for some weeks. A new structuring of the National Council of the Churches of Christ had changed the character of the Christian Medical Council and he would no longer be its secretary. The position he had been offered instead was one which it had been thought would please him. He was to work with one of our closest friends, Dr. Eva Weddigen, the one we always turned to when the family needed medical attention, as good a doctor as ever took the oath of Hippocrates. But there were reasons why Fred did not wish to accept the new position.

For the first time in his life, he looked old, beaten. Judy, Vicki, and I could hardly believe that this was the man who had sustained us and had taken philosophically wars, concentration camp, and back-breaking days and nights in mission hospitals.

"What will I do?" he asked pathetically. "I've never looked for a job in my life."

"God has led us every step of the way so far," I reminded him.

His most difficult task at the moment was to keep his wife and children from feeling bitter. "You don't understand," he would say, again and again. "You just don't understand."

"I understand all right," Vicki said to me when we were in her room alone. "He doesn't blow his own horn enough. He never has. Those people don't know what a good man they've got. You have to keep tooting to get ahead these days. He's so darned naïve."

"That's not it at all, and you know it," Fred said when I told him.

Both girls showed him their love in all the small experiences of the day. The other children phoned often and wrote long, encouraging letters.

Christmas was a dark, foggy day; only dirty patches of snow remained on the ground. We were as downcast as the weather. But the four of us were drawn very close to one another as we celebrated the birth of Christ under these strange circumstances. We discovered that Christmas did not have to be a happy one to be blessed. This time we were really celebrating "Christ's Mass."

As soon as the rumors of the National Council's changes

got around (Fred had sworn us to secrecy), and long before
the changes were announced publicly, requests for Fred's
services began to pour in. They were challenging opportunities, and he was encouraged by so much confidence in his
abilities, but he could not come to a decision.

"The world is wide open before us," I told him. "Accept
any one you want, Taiwan, any of them. We'll go where you
feel like going."

"I felt called of God to leave the overseas work for the
Christian Medical Council," said Fred. "Now I am only a
pawn on a board."

"But a loving Father has His hand over that pawn," I told
him, "and He will move it to exactly the right position."

"Waiting for Him to move is always the hardest, isn't
it?"

"We ought to know. But 'they that wait' *do* 'renew their
strength.' "

"I should be Hercules," he said.

Actually, the waiting period this time only seemed long. In
a matter of days, Dr. Theodore Stevenson, United Presbyterian Medical Director for the overseas program, requested
Fred's transfer back to his own denomination as Ted's Asso-
ciate. Nothing could have pleased Fred more. We both knew
it was the right move.

"I, who thought I was so completely ecumenically minded
—and I still am—feel as if I'd come home," he said, a few
weeks later. "And I have yet to find a medical policy on
which Ted and I disagree." He was young again, working
with his usual zest and enthusiasm.

XX

Thanksgiving, 1965, was as gloriously happy as the previous Christmas has been sad. Vicki was the first of the clan to arrive. It was good to get home from work that Tuesday night and find dinner ready. We could have guessed that the *pièce de résistance* would be "Vicki's Exotic Hawaiian Pork Chops."

"What did you put in them this time?" I asked.

"Don't tell us," said Fred. "I'd rather not know." We both agreed that they were delicious. Different, but—well, delicious.

We heard very little that evening about Vicki's radio and television major at the University of Tulsa, Oklahoma (she had transferred from Tusculum College in Tennessee in order to get the required courses). What we learned was that the most wonderful man in the world was named Jim Harris—James Hewitt Harris, to be exact.

"I want to tell you all about him before Judy comes," said Vicki. "It looks as if I may be married before she is, and if I were the older one, it sure would make me feel awful to have that happen."

"I wouldn't worry too much about that," said Fred. "Has he asked you to marry him yet?"

"Daddy! Of course not! I've only been out with him a few times.

"He has a real Irish sense of humor."

"He'd have to have, to marry you," said her father.

We liked what we heard of James Hewitt Harris. One thing was certain—our Littlest One was deeply in love.

We defrosted the refrigerator, stuffed the turkey, and put away thirty-three dollars and fifty-six cents worth of groceries without batting an eye. We could afford it for the first time in our lives.

Back to work all day, then home to the house exploding with children, hugs, laughter, and calls of "We thought you'd never come!" "Don't you two ever take a day off?" "How long before you'll be ready to eat?" This last from Jim's wife, Dixie, who had brought the dinner for all of us—beef burgundy, rice, and all the fixings, cooked on her new range in their new home on Long Island.

Our oldest son, Jim, at age thirty-three, had chosen his bride with no help from his threatening mother. He and Dixie were working on the same paper in Elmira, New York. "I figure that, next to Mom, I'm the biggest worrier in the family," he wrote us, "and I'm not going to miss marriage, the world's best opportunity for worry." They were married on May 4, 1963, and we had the fun of another family wedding. "Tom and Janene really gave me the idea," said Jim. "I figured that when my baby brother got married, it was time for me to get busy."

"Now, Jim, come on, tell them how it really happened," said Dixie.

"Well, to tell the truth, it took the Cuban crisis to scare me into it," said Jim. We never did hear "how it really happened." We were just terribly glad that it had.

"Do you remember the first time Jim ever brought you here?" I asked Dixie.

"Do I? I was terrified," she replied. "The Scovel family is an awful lot to take all at once."

"I knew everything was all right when you and Jim were in the kitchen doing dishes. Jim had started his usual teasing. You stopped washing, put your hands on your hips, looked him straight in the eye and said, 'Scovel, you have so much to learn.' "

Jim had successfully passed the examinations, judging from the look in their eyes now.

"We'd better go ahead and eat. There's no telling when Judy will arrive," said Fred.

"Here, Mom, let me fix you a plate," said Dixie.

I sat at the small table with our grandchildren. Helen did not look like either Carl or Faith; she was a very separate little individual. David's hair was the most beautiful auburn I had ever seen. He was reading books, "all by myself," he told me. The two cousins enjoyed being together. "We're both five years old," said Helen, "but Chris is only three." Christopher, Helen's brother, was a Greeley, and resembled Faith's father. We all thought he looked like English royalty. But he had the ingenuity and energy of a regiment of Gurkhas. "He comes by it naturally," I told Fred as he refilled my plate. "Look at his father and his grandfather Scovel." Every little while, Chris would stop in the midst of some impishness to run over and kiss—very gently—little blonde Jessica, the one-year-old daughter of Jim and Dixie.

I couldn't help thinking how fortunate these children were to have been born in a country where they could have enough to eat and every opportunity to grow to be normal, healthy men and women; and that they had always been surrounded by love.

A storm of protest arose over Jessica's being put to bed, so Carl gathered the rest of the brood at one end of the room, where they sat on the floor for the inevitable "lion hunt"— ". . . up the little mountain, down the other side, around the tree, through the river . . ." faster, faster, faster.

"Do it again, Daddy," said Helen.

"No more," said Carl, breathlessly. "Nai Nai will read you *The Little Red Lighthouse and the Great Grey Bridge.*" They snuggled beside me on the long couch as I read.

At last they were all kissed good-night, and it was suddenly quiet.

Judy had still not arrived. "I'll bet we get a telegram from North Carolina," said Jim.

"Or Alaska," said John.

"Don't worry, Mom, she'll be all right," said Anne, who from her earliest childhood in China had calmed my fears. But Judy could get lost more often and more easily than anyone we knew. She had probably taught until noon, and may have had a Thanksgiving party for her elementary school pupils later. But Williamson, New York, was only five or six hours away and she had hoped to arrive in time for supper. At ten o'clock she drove in.

"Judy, where have you been?" I asked.

"Hohokus," she replied, trying to make a joke of it.

"How in the world did you ever get to Hohokus?" asked Fred. "That's south of Stony Point, in New Jersey. You were coming from the north."

"If I knew how I got there, I'd have been here two hours earlier," she said. "Is there anything left to eat?" Faith, a good sister-in-law to have at hand, was off to the kitchen at once.

"I'm so tired," she said when we were in her room. "The fog was awful. Oh, it's so good to be *home.*"

Judy had worked through all her vacations from Western College and had then gone to Ithaca College to complete her Master's degree in Music Education. This was her second year of teaching. She loved the school, the children, the town of Williamson and its people. And she loved especially the children of the migrant workers who came every year to pick

apples. But it broke Judy's heart that she could do so little for
them. "The hardest part of it is, I can't be a mother to them.
We teachers are their first contact with the world, and the
world is going to be tough on these kids. We have to expect
the best from them and hold them up to standard until they
produce their best. It sure is hard when you want to take
them in your arms and cry with them."

Tonight she was showing the strain. "I have to decide
about next year, too," she said. "Am I going to stay on in
Williamson or go to Lebanon or Egypt or some other place as
a missionary?"

"You're going to eat your supper and have a happy
Thanksgiving," I told her.

❧ XXI ❧

Back in the living room everyone was talking and the TV was going full blast.

"Shall I turn this thing off?" asked Fred.

"No," two or three of them shouted.

"But you're not listening to it."

"I am," said Vicki. "Let's have it on, please? You men will have it all day tomorrow for your stupid football."

The males in the family visibly brightened. I remembered Janene orienting Dixie on marrying a Scovel. "He'll be wonderful to you until football season," she had said. "Then you might as well forget you have a husband."

"Speaking of football games," said John, "did your daughter tell you what she did when I took her to Princeton to see the game?"

Anne groaned. "Please don't listen to him," she said.

"Go ahead, let's hear it," said Jim.

"Well, I'd saved up my hard-earned cash and off we went to the Dartmouth game. And just at that hush, when everyone is waiting to see whether or not it's a first down, Anne pipes up with 'How many home runs does Dartmouth have now?' "

The story could have been apocryphal—or not. The laughter completely drowned out the last of the Danny Kaye show. Anne's protests continued through the commercials.

"Be quiet, everybody," said Vicki. "Here's Jim Hartz on the late news. I met him at Tulsa. He's a doll."

Quiet was a collective impossibility for the Scovel clan. When the news was over, and Vicki flicked off the switch, I told them about being taken to Saratoga to hear Galli Curci sing because this would probably be the only opportunity I would ever have to hear an opera singer. I never forgot the experience. I had not known that it was possible for the human voice to produce such music. And when we were engaged, Fred took me to Carnegie Hall to hear the Philharmonic. All those instruments making such harmony that heaven filled the hall!

Our children could be having an argument, wandering about the room, or strumming guitars and ukes while the orchestra was playing, but they could also stop suddenly and ask, "What on earth is the matter with that oboe?"

The conversation dwindled until the subject of Vicki's marriage arose.

"She's trying so hard not to say too much," Judy whispered to me. "I wish she'd loosen up and be herself. I want to hear all about him."

The two ministers in the family were pretending to vie for the honor of performing the ceremony. "We'll worry about that when, and if, the times comes," said Vicki. "Why don't you work on Judy? She'll be married before I am."

"How about it, Judy?" asked John.

"Not me. I think every family should have an Auntie Mame and I've volunteered."

"Auntie Mame was happily married. To a multi-million-aire," said Vicki.

"Now you're talking," said Fred.

"Let's get down to business," said Carl to Vicki. "I'll give you a twenty-dollar wedding, complete with one year's counseling."

"I'll do better than that," said John. "My ten-dollar wedding includes one baptism."

"We Scovels tend to marry conservative people," said Judy. "They are all the same pattern. I'm going to marry a whirling dervish astronaut."

"Isn't the astronaut a little Scovelish?" one of us asked.

"Right. I'm going to marry a whirling dervish."

Somebody had made coffee and it was now being served with Anne's delicious apple pie. We were getting our second wind and might be up all night.

"Mom and Dad, did you know we'd filled out preliminary papers for going overseas?" asked Anne.

"We're not at all sure about it, so don't get your hopes up," said John.

"What do you mean, 'Don't get your hopes up?'" I asked. "The world is the mission field. Jim is doing important work on *Newsday* and he's no farther away than Long Island. Tom and Janene happen to be in Thailand. Being a missionary is being where God wants you to be at the time He wants you to be there."

"You certainly felt that way, John, when you left a successful pastorate to teach Woodworking and Electricity to the fellows who need it in Trenton High School," said Fred.

"But weren't you just a little proud when Tom decided to be a missionary?" Faith asked.

"Oh, I don't know," Fred replied. "We were glad we hadn't done anything to discourage him by being missionaries ourselves."

"I'll have to admit that when I open that *Yearbook of Prayer* and read, 'Scovel, Frederick G., M.D.' and under it, 'Scovel, Thomas S.,' I *do* get a thrill," I added. "And I'll never be able to tell you how thrilled I was the first time I heard Carl preach. But then, I'm thrilled when I hear Judy play, and I could go on from there with all of you."

"What's this about *your* being a missionary, Judy?" asked Carl.

"Yes, tell us what made you decide," said Faith.

"You know you can't explain to anybody why you want to a missionary," said Judy. "There isn't a thing about it that makes sense."

"But you're certainly carrying on a mission to those kids in Williamson," said Vicki. "Why do you want to change?"

"Tom asked me the same question. I wrote him that it wasn't any great, noble call; it was just that I didn't think I'd ever be satisfied until I'd given it a fling. Maybe I want to go because it's harder to carry out your mission here in America than overseas."

"I should think it would be the other way around," said Dixie.

"Tom didn't agree with me, either. He said it was harder overseas because there were fewer places to escape to."

Could I face having her go alone to that difficult mission in the Near East? Fred and I had seen too much of the stark loneliness of single missionaries. It was different with married people who could talk things over and who were facing difficulties together. But a teacher in a girls' school in Egypt—or in almost any of the missions around the world—would be expected to live under the constant scrutiny of her students; she would sleep in the same dormitory, play games with them in her off-duty time, take them to church and bring them back. Anything less would be considered a lack of dedication to her calling. Given free time of her own, where would she go for recreation?

We had seen it all over the world. The "single women" (God forgive us the label) lived together in one dwelling, ate at the same table, and often worked in the same building, however incompatible their natures might be. And many times, even those of us who were having difficulties adjusting

to married life—although we had chosen our own partners—
were heard to express doubt as to the spiritual commitment
of a woman who "just couldn't seem to get along with the
others." There was no way for us to prepare Judy for what
she might meet.

Father Scovel's verse came to me very clearly; it had sustained him while we, his children, were going through wars
in China. "I know whom I have believed, and am persuaded
that he is able to keep that which I have committed unto him
against that day."

"They're a wonderful family," said Fred as we went to bed.
"Where did they ever come from?"

"As you would say, 'Haven't the foggiest notion,' " I replied. "And they're so much fun now that they're grown up.
I thought the fun was all going to be over when they stopped
being little. But I enjoy them so much more now—no disci-
pline problems, no worrying that I'll do the wrong thing and
spoil their whole lives."

"All we have to do now is sit there and watch their minds
work," he said.

✎ XXII ✎

Late as it had been when we went to bed, nobody could sleep on Thanksgiving morning except Vicki, who slammed the door and put a pillow over her head. The grandchildren were up; bathrobed adults filled the small kitchen—warming milk, making toast, sleepily sipping coffee. At last, everyone was dressed including Vicki.

As the smell of roasting turkey filled the house, it became a dynamo of activity. Fred, Jim, and John went downstairs to get Cousin George and Harriet's big dining room table with all the leaves. Where was the tablecloth, the large white one? Where *was* the large, white tablecloth? Anne had had it for a church reception. Never mind. Get the crotcheted one Aunt Jen had given us. And the candlesticks Dixie had brought. Judy, get some autumn leaves from the garden. Boys, take *all* the children to Stony Point park. Not you, Carl. You and Faith go and get the ice cream. Who wants to do the salad? Who's a good cutter-upper? Where's the sour flifter? (This from Judy.) "Well, some people call it a flour sifter."

"Mom, come here a minute." It was Carl with Faith.

"I thought you'd gone for the ice cream."

"We came back in to tell you something, but you must keep it a secret," said Faith.

"Dad, you've got to hear this, too," said Carl. "You tell them, Faith."

"Oh, well, it's just that you are going to be grandparents again, in June."

Faith was radiant as she and Carl ran back across the lawn, hand in hand. What a day for giving thanks!

Back to the kitchen. Where were the sweet potatoes? Surely there were three cans of them. There were four cans of them. During one of those unexplained silences that settle on a group, Judy said, "Isn't it too bad that Cousin Harriet couldn't come."

No celebration was complete without Cousin Harriet, widow of our beloved Cousin George Allen, "sister" to Fred and me, and second mother to our children. We all knew what Judy was thinking. We were all thinking of the last time Cousin Harriet had been with us. The whole clan, including Brother Bob, Dorothy, and their children, had gathered to say farewell to Tom and Janene. The crowd being too large for the house, we had dinner that time in a private dining room at a family restaurant overlooking the Hudson, a mile or so from home.

After a delicious chicken dinner, accompanied by the usual intramural heckling, Carl led us in a service of worship. He used the Bible verse Father Scovel had given to me when I became a member of his church—"The Lord shall preserve thy going out and thy coming in from this time forth and even forever more." Then Tom and Janene had driven off in a shower of courage and confetti. They would be all right. They were together.

Could I be as brave if Judy left, alone? I watched her now as she amused the girls with the tale of her first production— an elementary school concert from *Sound of Music*.

A door banged open. "Grandma, we're hungry," called David from the back stairs.

"Just a few minutes more," I said. "Everybody out of the

kitchen while I take up the turkey and make the gravy."

"Let's have our little service first," said Fred. "We want you with us."

Silence, as Fred read the President's proclamation. Then John read from the 107th Psalm. Anne leaned over and whispered, "The same passage I have marked in my Bible 'January 25, 1951—Folks out of Communist China.' And John didn't even know it."

"Then they cried unto the Lord in their trouble," John read, "And he lead them forth by the right way, that they might go to a city of habitation."

How many miracles had it taken to bring this table full of people to this moment? There were those deliverances we knew nothing about and there were those of which we had been fully aware. The miracles that went into the children's education alone were worth the proclamation of a special thanksgiving day—the friend who had "felt led" to send us a semester's tuition at the moment when Carl thought he'd have to leave Oberlin and go to work; the estate left by my beloved Uncle Jim and the larger one left by one of Father Scovel's parishioners to be used "for his grandchildren's education." This bounty fell into our laps when the last three were in college at the same time. These were miracles that "just don't happen," but they had happened.

Carl was praying for Tom and Janene. If I cried, the tears were tears of joy. We kept our heads bowed while little Helen asked the blessing:

> "Our Father,
> who feeds the small sparrows
> and gives us bread,
> please feed all our brothers.
> Amen."

Then pandemonium broke loose once more. "There never was such a turkey." "Have you heard the one about . . . ?" "Just a little more of that delicious stuffing, Dad." "I'll get more gravy."

Judy caught my hand as I brought sweet potatoes to the serving table beside her father. "Daddy, do you remember what you said two Christmases ago when we were at Anne's?" she asked.

"Haven't the foggiest notion," said Fred. "What was it?"

"The floor was covered with tissue paper, toys, and toddlers. Carl had Helen on his back and was playing horse. Jim and John were running David's new train. You put your arm around Mom, as we three sat on the couch, and said, 'Darling, this thing sure snowballed, didn't it?' "

ACKNOWLEDGMENT

Special thanks are due to Judy. After her evacuation from Egypt following the Arab-Israeli War, June 5-11, 1967, she gave invaluable help with the manuscript while at home awaiting her reassignment to Iran.